T0171627

YOU CAN'T GET IT

Let Go of Fear—
You Are More in Control than You Think

TINA ANDERSON

BALBOA.
PRESS

A DIVISION OF HAY HOUSE

Balboa Press books may be ordered through booksellers or by contacting:

Balboa Press
A Division of Hay House
1663 Liberty Drive
Bloomington, IN 47403
www.balboapress.com.au
1-(877) 407-4847

ISBN: 978-1-4525-0717-0 (sc)
ISBN: 978-1-4525-0719-4 (e)

Printed in the United States of America

Balboa Press rev. date: 11/12/2012

To my precious children.
You make this journey so much more
than it ever would have been.
Your strength gives me strength every day.

To the divine loving universe.
Your love sustains me!

*It's the heart afraid of breaking
That never learns to dance.*

*It's the dream afraid of waking
That never takes the chance.*

*It's the one, who won't be taken
Who cannot seem to give,*

*And the soul afraid of dying
That never learns to live.*

The Rose

CONTENTS

PREFACE

About a decade ago I discovered that I could talk to the universe and more importantly, it could answer me back. I started with a pendant but before long I was in regular conversations with mother/father god and two spirit guides, via yes/no answers given by specific movements of my head whilst meditating.

The change that brought to my life has been subtle and yet sometimes overwhelming. Despite being an avid reader of spiritual books, I was not prepared for the challenges that would come whilst communicating with such intelligence. Regardless, it has been both a humbling and exciting experience.

On a personal level I am honored and very grateful. I am grateful that I no longer know the fear of death, the fear of scarcity or the fear of being alone. The only one I am afraid of now is myself. I acknowledge that I am in control of the situation at all times but I also acknowledge that sometimes I throw a curve ball, just for the challenge.

This book was written in about 8 hours but it has taken many more years of editing and questioning to be able to publish this simple truth about how the world works and how you can work within its natural laws to create exactly the life you want and need.

The reason you have come into this life is so simple and beautiful. The laws that operate within this reality are also simple and beautiful. In fact, they are so simple and beautiful that you just can't get it wrong. This universe has the potential to offer you anything you want and you have the ability to take it. You just have to know how.

I have received so much joy and compassion over the last decade from this all- loving intelligence. I hope you will find your truth in these writings and that you will also find the peace, synchronicity and love that I see in the universe every day.

Many Blessings

Tina Anderson

CHAPTER 1

THE LAW OF RELATIVITY

Picture yourself in the following situation. It's a cold, wet, windy day, and you have been caught out in the rain. It has soaked through your clothes, and your bones feel as if they are made of ice. You are starting to shiver, and your teeth are rattling. You are really, really cold.

You've all been there, whether you were a tradesman on a miserable winter day or were on your way home from work and got caught in the rain. Or maybe you are one of those super-fit adventure types and actually brought this on yourself by kayaking down the river in winter. However you got there, it is really unpleasant.

Now picture yourself arriving home and stepping straight into a glorious, hot shower. As the steamy water runs over your head and down your back, the heat slowly thaws your insides. Goose bumps appear all over your body. This shower could even rival an orgasm for the sheer joy and pleasure you feel in those first few moments.

We take a shower nearly every day of our lives. We have had hundreds, maybe thousands, of them, but nothing feels like the one you take when you have just spent several hours being very cold.

If we think it through, this situation is exactly what life is about. It is a great example of why we are here and how this universe works.

Why does this particular shower feel so much better and bring me so much more joy than my normal shower, which I have every morning before I start my day?

The answer is relativity.

The meaning of life is relativity.

Nothing more, nothing less!

Relativity. The only reason that particular shower was so good was because the circumstances that preceded it were judged to be so bad. So one could be thankful for such a wonderful warm shower, but the truth is one should also be thankful for being caught in the rain. It is a profound fact that without the "negative" being so intensely negative, we would not have had the opportunity to experience that rush of pleasure and joy that came in the initial moments of that shower.

So the question needs to be asked: Was getting caught in the rain and almost freezing to death actually a negative if you love the feeling of goose bumps and warmth spreading all over you under a hot, steamy shower? How could the cold, in that situation, actually be a negative? If we were to get out and put on a nice, warm dressing gown, watch a bit of TV, have a hot coffee, and then get back in the shower an hour later, there is no way we would have the same experience.

This law of relativity is evident everywhere you look. It is why we appreciate our lives so much more only after we have experienced a close call with death or overcome a dire illness. It is why "makeup" sex is so great. It is why the parent of the standard C-grade student is delighted to see a B and yet the parent of a straight-A child is disappointed to see B's on his or her child's report card.

I could go on, but I am sure you get the picture. It all revolves around relativity.

For every conceivable positive in this world there is a negative, and to make it even more interesting, whether it is deemed a negative or a positive changes with every person, in every circumstance, every time.

So the *potential* for positive and the *potential* for negative are represented in every person or situation.

For the most heroic acts in the world, of great sacrifice for humanity, there are also the most despicable acts the human mind can conceive.

That is relativity.

So lets move on and see what relativity has to do with why we are here and how this universe operates.

CHAPTER 2

LET THE GAMES BEGIN!

Before we go any further, we have to agree on one assumption, namely that there is life after death. Almost without exception, every religion in the world agrees that the body is not the sum of us and that our soul exists separate from our physical form. Religion also agrees there is a universal force, whether you call it God or something else, that interacts with this reality. We are all one with this force, we came from this force, and we will return to this force. Like a cup of water from the ocean, we are part of the eternal God force.

There are literally thousands of books written by psychics, mediums, and philosophers—not to mention all the writings of our mainstream religions—that lend evidence to the truth that there is a spirit form of every human being. I personally know this to be true. Twice in my life, when least expecting it, I have caught sight of an apparition, a person in spirit form. On one of those occasions, I actually walked right into it and then fell through it. That was an unnerving experience to say the least!

It is sufficient to say there is an "other side," where the spirits reside and the God force exists. Its most common name is heaven.

Now this is where I break from many traditional religions, primarily because I do not believe in hell. Nor do I believe in the devil or evil spirits.

In addition to there being no 'hell' on the other side, there is also no judgement. We do not have to earn our way back into heaven. It is our God-given right to go home. Every one of us goes home, no matter how badly we appear to mess it up while we are here.

Just think about that for a moment. This concept alone can bring more peace into your life. There is no hell! There is no one to judge you! There is nowhere scary and frightening for you to potentially spend eternity if you make a mistake! Hell only exists in one place, and that is here. This is hell. You are living in it!

How much of a hell this place is for you depends entirely on how you wish to view your reality.

The interesting part is that God, the universe, whatever you wish to name this universal energy, created this hell. So it has to be asked why an all-loving universe would create a hell in the first place.

Let's think about it. Imagine being in heaven. You come from there, so it shouldn't be too difficult. Heaven is all about love. Everything is cool. Everything is great. You can't be hurt, you can't die, and you don't have heartaches or tears. From everything I have ever read, seen, or felt, heaven is a place where nothing goes wrong and nothing is bad.

Ahh, a place of no relativity!

So what could be the problem with having a place to live eternally where there is no relativity? Well to start with, no orgasmic showers!

If we need a negative to accentuate a positive, what must be lacking in heaven is the relativity to create the extreme positives. There would be no challenges to help you define yourself. No stimulation or situations that give you the opportunity to show what you are made of. It would be hard to define who you really are and what you believe to be your truth.

So the universe created a place where we, as eternal spirits, could go to experience relativity, a place where we can experience ourselves being ourselves, defining who we are and what we believe to be right. And we, being either crazy, stupid, very brave, or just plain curious (or a combination of all), we—that is, you and I—volunteered to come here.

It's as uncomplicated as that.

A boot camp for the spirit world!

A virtual reality game of relativity.

This reality is simply a place of relativity provided for us to experience. In this place is the *potential* for anything and everything, all the perceived good and all the perceived bad. A reality made available simply to experience relativity. That's all—just experience.

There is nothing you have to accomplish.

There is nothing you have to achieve.

There is nothing God wants from you while you are here. It is challenging enough just being here. Even more fascinating is there is nothing you *have* to change or fix. In the end, we all go home.

Let me say that again. We *all* go home!

You do not have to earn admission into heaven. There is no such thing as someone going to heaven and another not. Every person you meet, see, or hear about will end up back on the other side. Everyone—"good" or "bad"—goes to heaven. I use those terms loosely, because we are not in a position to understand who is good and who is bad, as we will discuss shortly.

In addition, we are honoured for coming here by those spirits still on the other side, and I mean really honoured by them. This must be the bravest thing a soul can do. You volunteered to come into a reality that has an ample supply of fear, anger, sorrow, pain, and negativity. You are a hero in the eyes of the universe. It does not matter how badly you think you have handled your life to date, because as far as the universe is concerned, you are a bona fide hero in every sense of the word. I cannot stress this point strongly enough. I have had my own personal experience to reinforce this idea, and it changed my perspective forever.

Firstly, I want to point out here that I am not a dream analyst. I am sure analysing dreams works for some people, but not me. I believe that nearly all dreams are simply your brain running amuck while you are off guard. Like an unsupervised kid in a lolly store, it just runs off thinking all sorts of stuff until you wake up and get it back under control. Most of the time, I can hardly remember my dreams within a few minutes of waking up.

I have, however, had one particular dream that was very different. This dream was so vividly clear in every detail. Six months later it was still clear.

In this dream I was walking around the corner of a building. It felt like a Roman colosseum or some historical building. I looked up and I saw a man who I immediately knew to be my husband's father. I had met this man once, very briefly, about fifteen years earlier. I remember thinking, *That's my father in law, I look a mess and I wanted to look so nice the next time I met him.* Pretty strange! I had no intentions of meeting him. He had passed away about ten years earlier. Neither would I expect to feel ashamed or humbled by this man. I did not know him.

In the dream he just silently walked towards me and put his arms around me to give me a hug. The English language does not have the words or vocabulary to describe the feelings that came over me. Even though there were no words spoken he communicated two things to me in what seemed like only seconds.

The first: I had never ever, ever done anything wrong. I had never made a mistake or misjudged something. I had literally never, ever done anything wrong!

That was so intense! I can still remember the awesome wave of relief that enveloped me. I had never done anything wrong!

The second: I was adored. Not liked, not just loved, I was absolutely adored and worshipped. I was worshipped like one would a hero who had travelled the seas for years in search of a remedy or cure that would save many lives. Absolute hero worship!

And that was it. It was over. I sat bolt upright in bed and just started crying. A wave of peace came over me as I sat there in the dark in the middle of the night. It was the most awesome experience I had ever had. I would never have thought emotions that strong could exist.

I feel love for my children, and I am sure you do too, but multiply that by thousands to get anywhere near the love that was exchanged with me in those brief seconds. There is nothing on this planet that can come close to the intensity of those emotions of love and support. I did not know it was possible to feel such unconditional love. I understand now why people who have had a near death experience often say that they cannot put the experience into words because it is impossible to do so. There are not the words available to describe to you how intense those emotions were.

The bottom line here is you have volunteered to come into a reality of relativity, and your only job, so to speak, is to experience that relativity and then return home to that place of absolute love and support.

That's all there is to it!

You can't get it wrong!

If we are only here to experience relativity, how can we possibly get it wrong? Does this mean you can hurt people without there being repercussions? No, it does not, but not for the reasons you might think.

There are natural laws that are operating in this reality, and they are here to help us while we are here experiencing relativity. These laws help us have some control on how our lives unfold and they guide the whole experience.

So, let's see how these natural laws work.

CHAPTER 3

PREFERENCES AND DESIRES

In chapter 1 we spoke about this place being a place of relativity, and in chapter 2 we explored the concept that we volunteered to come into this place of relativity.

Now, there are many different opinions on what we are supposed to do or achieve while we are in this life. Many believe we are growing our soul or learning lessons. Some believe we are trying to make our way, over many lives, to another level of some type. Some religions believe we are earning our next life's reincarnation. However, as I mentioned previously, I don't think there is anything in particular we are here to do other than just experience relativity.

There is no more reason to come into this reality than there is to play a video game. It is simply for the experience.

It sounds so easy when you say it, but relativity hurts. Pain, suffering, loneliness, hunger, cold, fear, insecurity—

these are all faces of relativity. These are the negative aspects of relativity.

As human beings, we are so hard on ourselves. We live in a constant state of fear and guilt. Fear of judgment, fear of failure, fear of dying, fear of loneliness, fear of pain, and the constant fear of "getting it wrong" and when we are not fearful then we feel guilt. Guilt for everything others (or we) have already judged as our failings so far. This guilt can go back as far as "original sin" in some belief systems. Like fear, it is deeply entrenched on a subconscious level.

We simply don't give ourselves enough credit for the fact we are simply surviving on a day-to-day basis in the most inhospitable reality imaginable. No wonder we are worshipped, respected, and adored from the other side. This is certainly one hell of a journey.

You are so brave just to have come into this physical world to experience relativity. If you do nothing more than survive it emotionally and go home, you are a winner and a very brave soul. That is the goal, to experience the many faces of relativity and then return home.

It's not an easy thing to do.

But if we have a look at why we have decided to come into this reality of relativity and how we operate within it, we may find it does not need to be as hard as it has been to date. An understanding of how the universe is operating can give you the opportunity to work within these natural laws. This can make your life considerably less painful and certainly more guilt free.

To operate effective within these natural laws, we need to understand how they work.

The first thing to note is that as we go about our life experiencing this reality of relativity we get the chance to form preferences. In fact, due to the available contrast in this life, we get to do this all day, every day. It is done automatically. Every time you encounter the positive and the negative of a situation or thing, your mind automatically forms a preference. I prefer this experience to that experience. It is no different when we form a preference over food. We have the opportunity to eat pumpkin and then we have the opportunity to eat chocolate. At that point our minds are capable of expressing a preference in our food tastes. Let's say chocolate. Let's take that concept a step further and experience many more different types of food. Now you are well on your way to experiencing a desire. I desire chocolate, I like chocolate, I want chocolate in my life. It is not something you have to state it is simply a desire you put out into the universe through having formed preferences automatically.

The longer we live in this reality, the more exposure we have to an extraordinary range of contrasting experiences, allowing us to make more and more preferences, which translate into sharper and sharper desires.

Now, here comes the best part! The universe is then ready, willing, and able to bring to us our sharpest desires. This is the most extraordinary thing about the universe. It is here to serve us on this journey and that which we desire the most; the universe will deliver to us. Hence the sayings

"Be careful what you wish for" and "Ask and you shall receive."

This concept applies not only to the individual on a personal level but to the community you live in, the country you live in, and ultimately the entire human population. Every moment of every day, we are creating preferences and desires that eventually manifest themselves into our reality. These lead to more desires, which our universe continually provides. So, ultimately, we co-create our own reality on a personal level and on a global level and we are forever expanding what we are, what we have, and what we are capable off.

This reality holds within it the *potential* for all that is and all that will ever be. Humanity is ultimately responsible for what experiences we attract to ourselves based on what our collective thoughts are. Our thoughts are evident by what we repeatedly have our attention on. Current experiences are then a reflection of what we, as people, believe ourselves to be.

And then, as soon as we create something, as is our nature, we then desire improvement, which virtually guarantees that the universe will continue to expand. Over time we get closer and closer to our desires until we obtain those desires. Then our new preferences, created from the relativity of the new situation, go on to create new desires.

The game is never over. It never ends. There is no end point where all your desires are met. Your new "perfect" reality will produce more preferences and hence more desires and on the game goes, never ending for all eternity.

So, while we are here experiencing the relativity to obtain our own definition of who we really are, we are also co-creating our own reality and participating in the creation of humanity's reality at the same time. It is pure genius really and all within our control.

The only problem is that humans have such power in their thoughts, words and actions that we often manifest into our reality situations that are not a true reflection of who we really consider ourselves to be.

If the universe created only what *we* thought were, our sharpest desires, then the world would probably be a really cool, peaceful place. After all, we would all agree we desire world peace. However, it is not quite that straightforward. In fact, nothing in the human psyche is straightforward. Observation has shown me that the real preference is rarely for peace. Peace can be boring.

Have you ever wondered why war games outsell much more peaceful games so outstandingly?

We are so fascinated by extreme weather events, dangerous sports, crime and murder shows, and all things aggressive. We can't blame world leaders for aggression when we prefer it in our own lives as well. Do you enjoy a really aggressive, close football match where both sides are pushed to the extreme and emotions are high? It is far more exciting than a polite, much less emotional game, is it not?

This is a universe of relativity that gives us the ability to make preferences, which over time become our desires.

Understanding how those preferences eventually lead to the circumstances in our lives means we can take more control of the people and situations that show up in our world.

CHAPTER 4

YOUR JOURNEY BEGINS

So, let's imagine you are a spirit on the other side. Sylvia Brown, a world-renowned psychic and medium, has penned several descriptive books about the other side including 'The Other Side and Back, A Psychics guide to the world beyond'. Many other writings from mediums and psychics tend to support her theories as well. According to Sylvia, the other side exists in the same form as here. Heaven is not up in the sky but here on earth, just like our reality but at a higher vibrating dimension. Sylvia goes as far as to suggest that the topography and geography are very similar to here, but the other side sits about one metre higher than us and vibrates at a much higher rate.

Sylvia talks about great halls, which hold the records of our life here on earth. Personally I don't know, and truthfully I don't care. I figure there will be enough time to work it out when I get back but it makes for some fascinating reading. The important point is that we do all exist on the other side and we live our lives not dissimilar to here but without the relativity.

A couple of years back I wrote a short story to try to capture the essence of being a spirit coming into this reality. I would like to share it with you now.

*   *   *

You are standing in a large room. There are people all around you. The mood is joyful and the air is filled with excitement mixed with a touch of apprehension. This is your farewell. You are going on a journey. All the people you love are fussing about and giving you messages of encouragement and support at your decision to make this incredible journey. You have thought about this for ages. You have researched and planned. You have made notes about the key experiences you wish to have, what stops you want to make on the way, and which route you wish to take. You are organised. In your mind, you are confident and very much looking forward to this journey.

You look to your left and there he is, your trusted friend and guide. There is no turning back from here. Your eyes meet. You both realise the seriousness of this journey.

As you stare into his eyes you know you are going to have to trust him, and better still, you know you can. You know that whatever happens on this journey, he will be thinking of you the whole way and doing everything he possibly can to help you. He knows what route you intend to take. He knows what stops you intend to make. He knows what experiences you intend to seek and of course when you will be back. He has to know all this, because the minute you walk through that door, you won't remember any of it!

And that's the way it is. You go on this journey knowing that you have a map, knowing that you have a plan. Knowing that everything you need on the journey will be made available to you. Knowing that there is a reason why you're going, but once you leave you will not be able to remember. Why? Because you are going on a fantastic journey to earth! And your friend, well he has trained some time for this. It is never easy being a guide for someone when they decide to go to earth. It is a very murky, negative place down there, nothing like here at home and it takes a lot of effort to try and communicate with the one that is on the journey.

You look around you one more time at all the souls you love so much, people that you have done this journey with before and people who will soon join you on your journey. There are a couple of people you know and love on the journey already, and you plan to catch up with them along the way—if everything goes to plan. You run over the details in your mind. You have already picked your parents and the family you will be born into. That should set up some of the circumstances you require along the way to stay on your path. You look over the crowd and see a beautiful female soul that is going to join you shortly in the reality of relativity. She is a very brave soul, and you feel the love in your heart as you remember that she has chosen to come into your journey as your younger sister. You admire her for the courage it takes to agree to go on this journey with a serious disability. She has chosen to experience a degenerative disease that will make walking impossible. She has chosen this path not only to experience the negativity of the situation for herself but to allow you to experience compassion and selflessness, as it will be your job to support her through her journey. It certainly will not be easy for her.

Why do we do this. You ponder the thought again. Down there on earth there are countless theories for why we do this. Many say there is karma involved, and many say it is to learn lessons. There is truth to these things, but the main reason we go back is to experience. To experience negativity and its many faces, in particular fear. Fear is something we simply do not know in this reality. How can we know fear when there is nothing to be afraid of? How can we know joy if we have not known sorrow? How can we appreciate love if we have never experienced an absence of love, and how can we recognise happiness if we have never know sadness? Never has knowledge been of use to anyone without experience to go with it. You can read mountains of books about what it would feel like to walk on the moon, but in the end only the experience of walking on the moon can tell you what it is really like. You laugh quietly as you recall a similar comment recently from a soul who just got back home and enthusiastically stated that you can read all the books you like on childbirth, but until you try it for yourself you have no idea.

The time is getting closer. It is now that you need to make your farewells. You wander slowly around saying good-bye to all your loved ones. They are cheerful and upbeat. Your journey to them is so very short. You know that it will seem much longer to you, because down there you have to deal with the concept of time. Here at home time is not linear. To them you will be back in the blink of an eye, armed with stories and experiences from the reality of relativity.

Farewells all complete, you and your chosen guide head through the beautiful gold doors. The excitement is building as you go back over all the work that has gone into this moment. As the doors close behind you, an angel comes forward and leads you to a sitting area. This is the last time you and your guide have together. There is not much left to say though, so you sit in comfortable silence for a while. The beautiful angel comes to address you. She is simply reiterating what both you and your guide already know.

"I remind you once more. Earth is an illusion. Matter is not solid. Everything is made of universal energy, same as it is here, but much more dense. You still have the ability to control that matter by thought as you do here. However, unlike here, where it is instantaneous, there is a delay mechanism down there on earth. This is for your own protection. If you could manifest instantly as you can here at home, you may experience serious problems due to the negativity down there. We wouldn't want you getting in a bad mood and killing your mother-in-law with just a thought," the angel reminds you, with a sense of humour. You need reminding. It doesn't matter how many times you go back this is the one thing you keep forgetting. You are in control. You can still manifest; it just takes heaps more effort.

The angel addresses your guide. "You have studied and trained to support your friend from here. You already know it is going to be difficult at times getting your point across, but the love you have for your friend will certainly help."

Then the angel looks directly at you and says, "You have all the love and support of all the beautiful souls here and the unending wellbeing of the universe. We remind you that you have all the tools you require to create anything you desire. We thank you for going on this journey as a co-creator with the universe. You know as well as we do that the universe cannot grow without desire and that desires cannot be formed until we know what we desire, and we can't know what we desire until we have experienced what there is to desire. On the plane of earth that you go to now, everything exists. There is hot and therefore there is cold. There is love, so therefore there is hate. There is joy, so therefore there is also sorrow. There is compassion, so therefore there is also a distinct lack of compassion. Basically, there is good so there is also bad."

You do know all this. You run back, for the hundredth time at least, in your memory some of the previous journeys you have done. You are fully aware there will be some very good times and very bad times. There are many things you are not looking forward to, but there are many you are. One of them is the rain. You have memories of rain. As it doesn't rain here at home, you have not experienced rain since the last time you were there. The wind on your face, that's another memory that comes to mind. Oh, and chocolate, the last time you were there they had just started developing chocolate for mass production. You remember that. On earth you have to eat. You have memories of the fine foods you enjoyed in your last life. This life should be all right. You have it in your plan to be relatively successful so fine foods are something you look forward too.

As you sift through past memories, the angel grabs your attention again. "Okay then, are you ready? Remember, if you get down there and don't feel you can go through with it, you have the first twelve months to just come home without any explanation. It's your choice. After that twelve-month period, it is as per the plan, and no copping out early or you will just waste this glorious opportunity to experience relativity."

You thank the angel and turn to your guide, who is giving you his last words of advice. "Remember, follow your emotions. When you feel good in your heart you are manifesting positively and you are moving towards what you truly desire, when you are feeling bad inside, you are manifesting negatively. Let your emotions be your indicator, and please, above all, do not forget to talk to me!"

"I won't," you reply, but deep down you know that as the years go by, the memory of why you are going there will start to fade. You know it is highly likely that you will forget about your guide, but at least until you are about five years old you will still communicate.

The angel interrupts your thoughts and reaches out to you. "Earth time is now!" she says. You step forward towards the next set of doors, and as they open you fall forward into a deep dark space. This space is getting tighter and tighter. All of a sudden you are feeling heavier and heavier. You remember this from last time. You hate this bit. The being born bit. You wish there was a nicer way to enter this place. You know you have to stay squashed in here for a while until you eventually will be pushed through a really tight tunnel until you abruptly come out into a cold, bright world. No wonder every soul cries from being born. After the love and comfort of home, it is certainly a rude awakening. Gravity sucks!

Your guide sends love after you and starts the endless task of watching over you. He wonders how long it will take you to forget him, and how long, if at all, you will finally remember him again. He wonders how often you will stroll off the path. He wonders how many times he will have to intervene to try and keep you on track so that you can experience all that you went down there to experience. Above all he prays that you will forgive him for anything he has to do to keep you going in the direction you chose to go. He already knows that there will be situations and circumstances that the universe will have to bring about that you will not appreciate at the time. Above all, he hopes you will remember to manifest positive things into your life. He is aware that many souls have a much harder journey than they ever planned because they get caught up in the negativity and find it almost impossible to manifest abundance and prosperity in their life. He hopes you will not be one of them. Life has begun and now the rest is up to you. "Good luck," he says.

*   *   *

Ultimately, you are in charge, and more importantly you have at least one spirit guide, who you chose to help you along the way. You also have a whole army of angels, loved ones, friends, and teachers on the other side who are there to help as well. They are your cheer squad. They go everywhere with you. They see everything you do and they know what is in your heart before you even do. So, don't forget to ask for help. Little children know they have invisible friends. Maybe it's time for you to remember that as well.

CHAPTER 5

REINCARNATION, PAST LIVES, AND JUDGEMENT

It probably warrants a brief discussion at this point about reincarnation.

I will never forget something my youngest child said, at about the age of three. This was before it ever occurred to me how the other side worked or whether we had ever been on earth before. We were standing in her bedroom and I commented on the fact I was busy running after three kids. She looked directly at me and said, "Well, when I was older, I had five kids." My older daughter and I laughed and I said, "When you get older you are going to have five children." She stomped her foot. "No! I said when I was older I had five kids. I don't have them anymore because I am here." I remember looking at her with confusion, not understanding what she was talking about, and I distracted her instead with something else. She stuck with this story for nearly two years. Every now and then it would come up. Today I understand she was talking about a past life experience, and given the opportunity again I would have had a fascinating conversation with her, no doubt. Never underestimate what can come out of the mouth of babes. They haven't totally forgotten yet.

Another personal example was when one of my nephews, again around three years old, was watching some workers fence a paddock on his property. He looked at his mother quite seriously and said, "I use to do fencing when I was here before, and we did it just the same way as they are." What can you say to that?

There are many writings about young children remembering information about their past lives. I recall an excellent documentary, based in England, that examined stories of very young children identifying graves and giving accurate details of how that person died. It is a fascinating area of study that I hope will reap results over the coming years.

Since I realised that we have most likely come back many times to experience this reality, I have not had a lot of exposure to really young children. However, I am sure there are many of you who could relate stories that have come out of the mouth of our youngest souls. Some of these young children seem to be old souls who may have come back many times. They exhibit a degree of maturity that does not seem normal for such a young child. I suppose at the end of the day, if we chose to come here once, what would stop us repeating the exercise?

Another interesting area of study connected to reincarnation is past life hypnosis. I personally have never experienced past life hypnosis, but I have read some fascinating stories of practitioners curing ailments. The theory is that some of our worst phobias, fears, and ailments can be a residue of sorts from a past life. For example, a young woman has a throat disorder that makes it very uncomfortable and difficult to breathe. Under hypnosis, the practitioner retrieves information about a past life where the young girl was attacked by a lion in Africa and had her throat ripped out. Having participated in the therapy, the young women's ailment disappeared. Is it possible? I think it is time our best scientists and minds took the possibility seriously and made the appropriate investigations to find out.

One of the best series I have read about past life hypnosis is written by Dr. Brian Weiss, including *Many Lives, Many Masters*. Dr. Weiss is a practitioner who became involved in these studies when questioning some of the results he received in his practice.

When you consider it, it makes sense to me that we would volunteer to come here and we would do it with eagerness and anticipation. After all, how can one experience forgiveness and what that emotion feels like if there is nothing to forgive? How can one experience joy fully when they have never experienced sorrow? I doubt very much if we sit around on a bunch of clouds in heaven contemplating our navel (assuming we have one) for the rest of eternity. That would be really boring, I would suspect.

This is a really important reason why it probably isn't wise to be discriminating. There is every chance that you have been male, female, black, white, disabled, rich, poor, healthy, sick, smart, stupid, and just about every type of person you can imagine. You may have had past lives in Europe, Africa, or Asia. Even the people living in the remotest jungles on the planet are still souls here, from heaven, experiencing relativity. The point is you don't know. You never know who you were in a past life, so don't discriminate against different types of people in this life. It may just be your desire to play that particular role next life around.

It is part of the exceptional tapestry that is this realm of relativity. Every different person and situation is represented, and we actively participate in providing that contrast, life after life.

It's also very important that we recognise that this universe created this reality out of love. It created this reality so we could truly know ourselves. God created "hell" so that we could truly understand heaven. This means that the universe is responsible for all the bad things that happen here simply because it is also responsible for all the good things as well.

This reality of relativity is a precious gift given to us and inspired by unconditional love. What we do with the concept of relativity is completely up to us as humans just being. The universe wants us to know ourselves as the best form of ourselves that we can be. It wants us to experience joy, so therefore it invites us to experience sorrow as well, so we can truly know that joy. "God created Heaven and Earth," and that includes the good and the bad. Relativity is God's gift to the souls that reside in heaven with him, on that higher vibrating plane, and we may choose to come back here and play as often as we wish.

There is a brilliant story I once heard. It tells of a sad little soul sitting under a tree. Another soul approaches him to find out why he is sad. "I wish to experience forgiveness and compassion but I have no one to forgive."

The older spirit gives it some thought for a moment and replies, "I will come with you so you can experience forgiveness and compassion. The only thing I ask is in the moment I strike you down, a part of you remembers that it was your desire for me to do so."

What a fantastic way of understanding that we do need negativity. Sometimes when we do wrong by people, or they do wrong by us, perhaps it was meant to happen that way so you could learn something about yourself. Perhaps you wanted to experience forgiveness, compassion and peace. Perhaps you reincarnated for that reason.

I have had so many experiences that I initially judged as bad, but then I learnt so much by going through those experiences, and some of them were so life changing that I can see how important they have been in my life. So many times, "negative" outcomes in my reality have transformed themselves to "get out of jail free cards" that I am astounded.

I have spoken to many people about circumstances in their lives that initially looked to be negative but turned out quite positive. One example was a friend whose house burnt down. She expressed to me that as much as it was really painful having the house and all her personal possessions burn, the outcome was for her family to move to a different area, and now they are much happier than they were before the catastrophe.

Take the time to investigate situations where you or someone else has had a serious event affect their lives, and so often you will see that something really quite positive came out of the so-called negative circumstances. It led you down another path or changed the way you understand yourself and the world.

The more we think about this the more it becomes apparent. We need to resist the need to judge the behaviours and actions of others, especially in relation to ourselves. Maybe your soul actually wanted a certain experience, or that experience took you closer to those desires you are manifesting. Or perhaps "negative" circumstances moved you away from something you were not going to be happy with long term. Maybe the circumstances became the catalyst for change that you needed. There are so many variables in the universe. Only you can know how you may have benefited from a situation that originally did not look positive.

We will return to the subject of judgement later in the book because once you understand the Law of Relativity and the Law of Attraction, the ability to not judge people or circumstances is the next most important concept to internalise.

CHAPTER 6

LAW OF ATTRACTION

Okay. If you can see, firstly, that you do come from a place of unconditional love and that you are only here to experience, then you can understand that through your own personal experiences, you can create preferences that lead to desires in your part as co-creator of our reality. You may then start thinking, "It doesn't matter what I do to people around me." You may take the attitude, "Well, it is only an experience and they will get over it." And you know what? To some degree you are right.

A little while ago I decided to read the *Bhagavad Gita*, the Hindu equivalent of the Christian Bible. There are some reputable English translations, which manage to retain the original poetry while getting the message across accurately. I must say, when I first started reading it, I was shocked. At the risk of over simplifying the text and insulting any Hindus, I would like to summarise the first two chapters.

We have a warrior on a chariot and he is about to go into battle with his enemy, except this time his enemy is his neighbour. It is a civil war type situation. The warrior is distraught over the fact that he knows and respects many of the soldiers he intends to slay. He drops to his knees and asks Krishna, "How can it be right to raise arms against thy neighbour?"

Krishna's reply is something like, "Get off your knees and don't be a coward. You call yourself a warrior and you wish to experience being a warrior, then you should be the best warrior you can be. Do you really think you can hurt them? They are eternal souls. The God force created them, like you. They cannot be hurt. Yes, their bodies can be killed. Yes, you can cause them pain, but that is an illusion, because they are eternal souls playing the same game you are. They, like you, will go home and all will be well!"

Well, that just amazed me. I thought he would go on about not hurting your neighbour, but he didn't. The interesting part is that he is right. You can't hurt a soul no matter what you do; you can only provide them with an experience. That soul may have had the belief there is glory in dying in battle, and hence you would actually be doing them a favour, allowing them to experience glory. You cannot permanently hurt any human being, because we are all spirits and come from a place of unconditional love.

Now, before we all run out and start operating with a "heaven doesn't care" attitude, we must consider a natural law, which can never been broken.

The Law of Attraction.

This is the same natural law that enables you to bring to yourself those things you desire. You have heard it so many times as "what goes around comes around." Many people call it karma. The bottom line is you attract what you put out.

Negative intentions directed at any person or situation will send out a vibration that will attract more of the same. Nothing is surer. This is not strictly karma. This is a vibrational reaction. Pure science. That which vibrates at the same rate attracts.

So, in addition to you not being able to accurately judge if someone has truly wronged you, you should not intentionally wrong other people, as those actions will come back around to you.

I can hear some of you saying, "No, I know that person did the wrong thing by me," but seriously, you really don't! Without the perspective of a lifetime you can never guess how that action will or has benefited you. Has it changed your direction? Has it made you stronger? Has it given you a clearer idea of what you really want in your life?

Has it helped you define your preferences? Has it helped you understand who you are or who you are not?

Secondly, the universe will take care of them anyway. If someone intentionally hurt you for no reason (as known only by the universe), then they in turn will find themselves in very hurtful situations with people treating them the same way they treated you. It is a vibrational rule of the universe. Like vibration will attract like vibration.

Dr. Wayne Dyer would say, "I can choose peace over this." It does not matter what wrong has been done to you. You can chose to accept it as the way of the universe, walk away, and trust that eventually it will result in a positive for you. Alternatively, you can dwell in the negativity of it all, thus attracting more negativity towards you.

I have a bookmark, published by Dr Wayne Dyer, that contains a short poem, believe to be written on the wall of Shishu Bhavan, the children's home in Calcutta, India, where Mother Teresa worked tirelessly to help the poor. I live my life by it. For me the understanding allows me to release all resentment, bitterness, and any thoughts of being a victim.

Anyway

People are often unreasonable, Illogical,
and self centred.
Forgive them Anyway.

If you are kind, people may
Accuse you of selfish, ulterior motives
Be kind Anyway.

If you are successful, you will win
Some false friends and some true enemies
Succeed Anyway.

If you are honest and frank,
People may cheat you.
Be honest and frank Anyway.

What you spend years building,
Someone could destroy overnight
Build Anyway

If you find serenity and happiness,
They may be jealous.
Be happy Anyway.

The good you do today
People will often forget tomorrow
Do good Anyway

Give the world the best you have,
And it may never be enough.
Give the world the best you have Anyway

You see, in the final analysis,
It is between you and God.
It was never between you and them, anyway!

CHAPTER 7

MANIFESTING ABUNDANCE

As we have just discussed, the Law of Attraction operates without bias or prejudice, without care of the circumstances—it just operates. All thoughts create a vibration, and the frequency of your vibration determines what you are attracting to yourself.

The universe is nothing more than a giant magnet sending to you, every minute of every day, more of what you are putting out. A fascinating book on vibrations to read is *Power vs. Force* by David R Hawkins. In his study of Applied Kinesiology, Dr. Hawkins has spent many, many years testing and understanding the vibration of energy in our universe. He says, "Millions of calibrations over the years of this study have defined a range of values accurately corresponding to well-recognised sets of attitudes and emotions, localised by specific attractor energy fields, much as electromagnetic fields gather iron filings." He has adopted classifications of energy fields to be easily comprehensible, as well as clinically accurate.

He is basically saying that every person, thing, thought, and feeling has a certain vibration and that he can measure that vibrational level. Very interesting reading!

Furthermore, scientists, more specifically physicists, are adding scientific proof to the theory that the human mind can control matter. Recent experiments have shown that when molecules are broken down to the very smallest possible particles, quarks, they change their appearance depending on the expectations of the viewer.

They also show that when you whack two of these quarks together at very high speed to break them down further, surprisingly, there is nothing there. Nothing but that "thinking non-stuff" that Deepak Chopra talks about, or, in other words, nothing but God. Physicists are hoping that the Large Hadron Collider near Geneva in Switzerland will help answer some of the fundamental questions in physics concerning the basis laws that govern interactions between matter.

Other tests are proving that all matter is connected. Atoms, which apparently can be trained, are trained in a laboratory to perform certain actions. When you separate the particles and tell one to perform the action, the other, though separated by space, will perform the same action.

Look, I am anything but a scientist, hence my vague description of what is very precise in nature. The point is, there are scientists currently working to discover how the universe is operating, at the most precise levels, and they are making some outrageous discoveries.

What the scientists are busy discovering is that the universal force holds all matter together. God is everywhere. No wonder the scriptures say, "God is within." Of course he is. He/she is holding all the molecules that make up your physical form together. The Universal force is everywhere!

The good news is the Law of Attraction works in positive as well as negative. In fact, the Law of Attraction is your very best friend. It is what gives you back the power in this reality of relativity. It is where the free will comes into it. It works both ways. If you spend time giving thought to positive, loving ideas and situations, by the Law of Attraction, you will attract positive loving situations into your life.

Basically, what you think is what you get. This is not a new concept. One of the earliest books that points towards this idea is *Think and Grow Rich* by Napoleon Hill. Traditionally considered a business "must read," it talks about the power of thought and how thought controls and creates your success. I had been noticing situations in my life that were strangely, and coincidentally, changed or remedied. However, until I read *Think and Grow Rich*, I had not realised the seriousness of the connection between what I had been pondering and what had actually eventuated.

Using the Law of Attraction is commonly called *manifesting*. Manifesting is a fascinating subject in its own right, and over the last couple years there has been a flood of information on the market that investigates manifesting and how it works.

Sales people have practiced manifesting for many years, disguised as positive affirmations. I am sure many of you have heard the theory of writing yourself positive notes and sticking them around the house to build confidence and success in your life. Well, they work, and they work really well. The reason they work is because of the Law of Attraction. As you read those notes you are putting a positive emotion or thought out into the universe, and the universe reacts the only way it can, by bringing that thought closer to you. The more positive emotion you attach to the thought, and the stronger you can visualise it, the more success you have.

Manifesting is the normal way of life on the other side. Apparently, we create houses and beautiful buildings on the other side, but we do it with thought alone. If we stand there and wave our arms around and imagine a spectacular building, it appears before our eyes. On the other side, we can turn water into wine and stones into bread, like one famous incarnation of a soul that has been to Earth before.

We can manifest here as well. However, in this reality, manifesting works much more slowly for most of us. Having said that, there have been examples of humans who have been able to instantaneously manifest in this world. Again, Jesus would be one of the most well-known examples, and he did say that we are capable of doing all that he can do. We knew we could when we arrived, but we have been caught up in the illusion of relativity and have forgotten our most precious skill.

The more you study this concept and the more you practice the principles of manifesting, the easier and easier it becomes.

A fantastic book on the subject of manifesting wealth, which was written years ago, is *The Science of Getting Rich*, by Wallace D. Wattles. You can usually find this book on the Internet, often for free. It is only about fifty pages long, but the wealth of knowledge in those fifty pages arguably makes it one of the most valuable books on the planet. It was originally written in 1910, and the principles outlined still apply today. Many of the books on manifesting we see published today refer back to this ageless classic.

Again, another wonderful book on manifesting is *The Power of Intention* by Dr. Wayne Dyer. Dr. Wayne Dyer is right up on my list of the most credible and wise human beings that has ever put pen to paper. In fact, my journey to this point started with a little book of his many years ago, called *Pulling Your Own Strings*. It has been quite some time since I read it, but it gave me the insight and strength to find my own path instead of following someone else's.

Esther Hicks is also a divine teacher who gave the world *Ask and It Is Given*, along with many, many other books that cover the art of manifesting. Her readings are priceless when it comes to understanding this natural law and how it works.

Finally, I must not forget Deepak Chopra, one of the world's leading authorities on the power of thought. What fascinates me about Deepak Chopra is that he found his way into this field of study from the path of an oncologist. Dr. Chopra had been a practicing oncologist for many years, and he often pondered the paths of those diagnosed with cancer. Why did some people with very, very serious cancer not simply curl up and die, as per the doctors expectations, and yet some patients with a so-called mild case of cancer would not live even three months. When a close friend of his died from cancer under unusual circumstances, he took it upon himself to investigate the connection between a patient's thoughts and their ability to heal themselves. Dr. Deepak Chopra has since written numerous books on manifesting health, wealth, and happiness, and I have always found much truth in his writings.

I give you these references because I am not going to spend chapters explaining how to manifest things into your life. As I said, there are countless books that can help you with the day-to-day stuff.

The bottom line is that you can create anything you want in your life. Love, happiness, great wealth, fantastic family, great social life, anything you want. You have the power. You had it at home on the other side and you brought it with you. You control your reality by your thoughts and you participate in the creation of all humanity with your thoughts. You have the free will to decide what comes into your life and what doesn't; however, there are some serious guidelines, which we will cover now, that need to be understood to ensure successful manifesting in your life.

CHAPTER 8

YOU ARE RICH!

Okay, let's start here. It is probably a very simplistic statement to say the universe is a very intricate force. However, the very preciseness, and the fact that the universe is so complicated, means that manifesting is not what it may appear to be on the surface. I was saddened to hear criticisms and speculations about the DVD *The Secret* when it was first aired on Channel 9 in Australia. Some of the feedback from radio presenters, and the general public alike, was very sceptical. As much as Rhonda Byrne and her team did a fantastic job, I can understand this scepticism given the challenges in presenting the Law of Attraction in a two-hour movie. It left as much to be answered as it explained. One Brisbane late night radio commentator I heard was laughing about his apparent ability to "just manifest a Ferrari into his life with very little effort." He was clearly sceptical. In many ways he was right, because unless you understand the full ramifications of manifesting, it is not quite that easy.

I personally have been consciously working with the Law of Attraction for the last fifteen years, and unconsciously my whole life, just like you. I first came across the concept when I was in business, before I had read anything about it. Since then, I have actively experimented with the Law of Attraction. Over the years, I have been delighted to read and hear many, many other opinions on the subject. As the saying goes, when the student is ready, the teacher will appear.

It is from this place of experience I will define, what I feel, are the most important points to consider. I will focus mainly on wealth, as I know money, wealth, and success are a high priority for nearly all Australians. However, the same principles apply also to love, marriage, and health. Whatever it is you wish to attract into your life.

The first point about wealth is the whole concept of wealth itself. Personally, I think this is the biggest issue for Australians. We need to simply let go of the battler mentality and move forward. Okay, we may have originated as a convict settlement, and yes there is an enormous amount of pride involved when we consider where we have come from, but look where we are now. It is of no benefit to continue, as a society, to believe that we are battlers or victims of uncontrollable circumstances. Australia is one of the richest countries in the world. So why are we hanging on to the battler mentality as part of our heritage?

We have one of the highest, if not the highest, success rates per head of population in sporting achievements worldwide. We have some of the planet's most brilliant scientists making breakthroughs in all areas of medicine and the environment. We have (whether you want to agree with me or not) intelligent politicians on both sides of the house who are well motivated and we have a generosity on a personal level that matches any country in the world, particularly in supporting charities and worldwide aid agencies.

By world standards, we are an incredibly wealthy country. We enjoy one of the best lifestyles of anywhere on the planet. I think the best, when you factor in weather. We are truly rich!

Now I know there are some of you probably groaning quietly to yourself and thinking, "I am definitely not rich." This is possibly one reason why you cannot see evidence of being rich in your life. I have thought exactly the same thing many times. I have felt the pressure of not being able to make ends meet. I have had my card declined at the supermarket, and I know that feeling of just getting by, week after week, wondering what trick you are going to pull to make everything work out and the electricity stay on.

It is so hard to feel rich when money issues on a day-to-day basis consume you, but I would like you to consider an African woman who has been widowed with four young children. She is squatting in front of her one bedroom hut talking with a journalist. He asks her to describe what she thought someone who was rich would have.

In your mind consider the changes that would occur in an African mother's life if she were to receive the following things, and at the same time be aware of how much you take them for granted:

- Oven
- Shower
- Toilet
- Bed
- Stove
- Car
- Lounge
- Television
- Bath
- Refrigerator
- Blender
- FOOD
- Fresh water
- Good cutlery
- Pushbike
- Telephone
- Computer
- Toothbrushes
- Blankets
- Warm clothes
- Make-up
- Towels
- Pillows
- Toilet paper
- Freezer
- Lights
- Heater
- Supermarkets
- Jewellery
- Hairdressers
- Books
- Stereo
- Dryer
- Shoes
- Education
- Microwave
- Washing machine
- Swimming pool
- Air-conditioning
- Vacuum cleaner

Now I say to you, if you have even a fraction of what is on that list, then you are considered rich, and it is about time you stopped thinking you are poor or broke or not getting by. I can't think of many people in this country who could seriously call themselves poor. Yes, we have some homeless people. This is one area of our society where I think we could seriously put some more effort into, because there really is no excuse for homelessness in Australia. However, nearly every single human being in this country has access to most of the items on that list and hence is rich by world standards. I could also add here that even for the homeless in Australia the situation is not that dire. I was in a situation where I had to ring Lifeline once, many years ago, because I had nowhere to stay, with a small child. I was stranded in Queensland and had only 20 cents to my name, enough for one phone call. I have to say, those people were so supportive and practical. They sorted me out, put me on my feet, and sent me on my way with no fuss at all.

Now, if you want to get this manifesting thing working, the first thing that you are going to have to accept is that you are already rich. By birth or design you are already in the lucky country and as such you are already rich.

There are seven billion people on this planet and it is a small percentage that has access to all the things we do. In a talk by Tim Costello, representing World Vision, he stated,

- There are six billion people in this world.
- One billion are rich.
- Four Billion are just getting by on about $5 per day.
- One Billion are dying from lack of fresh food and water, living on under $1 per day.

Here is another beautiful little reminder of
just how well we are doing:

<u>We are blessed</u>

If you woke up this morning with more health than
illness, you are more blessed than the million that will not
survive the week.

*   *   *

If you have never experienced the danger of a battle,
loneliness of imprisonment, the agony of torture, or the
pains of starvation, you are ahead of 500 million people in
this world.

*   *   *

If you can express your beliefs without fear of harassment,
arrest, torture, or death, you are more blessed than almost
3 billion people in this world.

*   *   *

If you have food in your refrigerator, a roof over your
head, a place to sleep, and clothes on you back, you are in
the top 75 per cent of the richest in this world.

*   *   *

If you have money in your bank and in your wallet and
some spare change in a dish, you are among 8 per cent of
the world's wealthy.

*   *   *

If your parents are still together and alive, you are very, very rare.

*   *   *

If you hold up your head with a smile on your face and are truly thankful, you are blessed, because the majority can but do not.

*   *   *

If you can hold someone's hand, hug them, or even touch someone on the shoulder, you are blessed because you can offer God's healing touch.

*   *   *

If you can read this message, you are more blessed than 2 billion people in this world that cannot read anything at all.

CHAPTER 9

MONEY AND YOUR BELIEF SYSTEM

When speaking about wealth we must address the topic of greed. Did you know that if you took all the money in the world and divided it equally between every man, woman, and child on the planet, there would be enough for every person to have $3 million dollars.

Yes, that's right, $3,000,000! Where is your share?

As far as I am concerned, you can't even consider yourself greedy until you have your $3 million!

You have to realise, money is only energy. These days it is not even backed up by gold as it used to be. Money, in the eyes of the universe, is exactly like everything else. It is energy vibrating at a certain level. The brass tacks physics of the situation is to get yourself vibrating at the same level as money and it will flow to you.

Once upon a time, I use to argue that there was no way I would ever buy a Ferrari. Imagine all the poor people you could feed in the world for the price of that car. And yes, you are right: you can, if that is what you want to experience. But you can also feed the families of the car salesman who sells the vehicle. Then he will spend some of it at his daughter's school, which will help them. You will also be supporting the families of the manufacturers in Italy and, with the trickle-down effect, some of the local Italian businesses as well.

The fact is the only way you can be greedy in this world is not to spend your money.

Do you hear me?

Greedy people are people who stop the energy from flowing. They are so scared that the flow will not continue (called a scarcity mentality) that they put it under their mattress or in a shoebox and take it out of circulation. They conduct business in an aggressive way that indicates there is not enough to go around, and they must succeed by taking from someone else. That is greed, because nobody can benefit from the money. Even if you put the stuff in a bank account, you are still moving it on, as the bank can lend it back out as a home loan or business loan. At the end of the day, as long as you keep the money moving, you can't possibly be greedy. It is more about your attitude to the money in the first place.

Additionally, don't feel you have to share your money with all who want you to. Money is a personal journey for all people. It is part of the journey. It is the arena in which we most commonly create challenges for ourselves. Personally, I would rather have my challenges in the financial arena than in the arena of health, family, or love.

You will meet people you want to share money with and those you don't. The decision should be guided by what you feel is right, whether it is a charity or a family member. The golden rule is never to give money out of guilt, only out of love. In fact, in a lot of instances, for example, people who win the lotto and give money to family members can actually see this backfire and cause many problems. The metaphysical explanation would be that the person was not vibrating at the same level as money in the first place. So, even though they received some, they could not keep it or make good of it, because they were not comfortable enough to do so. We have to learn to become comfortable with money for it to flow towards us. We have to rid ourselves of much of the guilt associated with having money, or we will just push it away, even if we win the lotto. Do you know that 95 per cent of lotto winners end up in a worse financial situation than before their win? Money won't stick with you unless you are comfortable having it, and if you feel greedy or unworthy of large sums of money, you will never stay wealthy.

I will add here, though, the more comfortable you become with money, and the more you understand the abundance of money, the more you will give away, because there is no feeling in the world as great as the feeling of giving when it really helps someone and you live with a real sense of "there is more where that came from."

There are many wealthy people who will attest to this. Oprah is one. She often says there is no feeling so good in her world as when she is in the process of giving. Now we all know Oprah tends to give in a really extravagant fashion, but giving in a very small way is just as powerful.

Giving does not have to be extravagant, nor does it have to involve money. Sometimes just doing the dishes for a heavily pregnant friend can be a profound help. Anything that makes it easier for one of our fellow human beings to cope in this realm of relativity is a blessing. Once again, as per the Law of Attraction, that which you give comes back to you many times over.

When it comes to manifesting money, your belief system is everything. The same applies to those of you wanting to find a person to love and those of you wanting to improve your health. As I said, I picked wealth as the example because it is one of the biggest areas of concern to the average Australian, which is quite ironic in the land of the rich.

You have to believe you can have your share and that you deserve it, and then the rest is easy. Wealth will be attracted to you in the best possible way that takes into consideration *all* other desires you are manifesting.

You have to accept that you are not being greedy. You have to really understand that there is enough to go around and that your success is not taking away from someone else. As Wayne Dyer likes to say, "You cannot possibly be poor enough to stop everyone else on this planet being poor, and you cannot possibly be sick enough to stop someone else being sick." It is an abundant universe and there is more than enough for everyone.

I ask you over the next couple days to pay attention to the conversations you hear around you. I don't think you will go a day without hearing someone, including yourself, say, "I can't afford that" or "we are always broke" or "I will never be rich" or "everything is so expensive these days." These thoughts are based in a scarcity mentality, and as such they vibrate at a very low level, bringing your vibration level down. You get what you say you will get.

As we said before, manifesting works because you put your thoughts out there and the universe complies. Words are just as powerful as thoughts; in fact, they are stronger, because you have vocalised them to someone else. Thoughts, words, images, movies, music, books, and conversation are all ways of manifesting. What you think, you are!

Like many wise men in the past have said, "Your mind is like a garden. You reap what you sow."

Spend some time listening to yourself and the people around you. Observe what thoughts and conversations are being put out for the universe to hear. What sorts of TV shows are on in your house? All drama shows are banned in my home. I figured there is enough drama in this world that can sneak into my life; I am not going to invite it in through the television as well.

Once I understood the power of manifesting, all medical programs and crime programs went on the banned list as well, and on some level I have always known not to watch horror movies. I hate them. I am not going to spend half an hour to an hour thinking about the murder of a child on a television show, or worse still, in a movie, when I have children of my own. Personally, I do not want my brain to be considering such thoughts, let alone vibrating at that level. I do not want to invite that level of strife into my reality.

The bottom line is, if you want to use the Law of Attraction to your advantage, then pay attention to what you may be attracting already.

Look around your life and be aware of thoughts like "that would be my luck" or "I always have bad luck" or "we are always broke." If you just start changing simple thoughts like those into positive versions of that thought, you will see changes in your life for the better. See money as a positive, higher vibrating energy that you can utilise yourself and share with the rest of the world. Money and spirituality are not opposites. In fact, people who do what they love the most often find the money follows.

Thoughts are simply vibrations put out into the universe, and they attract a similar vibration back to them. This is why sometimes you can be having a good day and suddenly you may have a negative thought. As you ponder that thought, it attracts more thoughts that vibrate at that level to you, so you have another negative thought, followed by another, and as many people will tell you, or as you may have experienced yourself, you can spiral right down to a really dark place in no time at all.

A similar thing happens in the positive. You may hear an uplifting song and start thinking an uplifting thought. A thought that is positive will attract more positive thoughts, and hence you can spiral up until you are genuinely in a state of joy.

This is why it is so important to stop a negative thought process in its tracks, by whatever means necessary. Play some music that makes you feel good. Maybe pick up an uplifting book and just open to any page and start reading. It will attract more positive thoughts in. Maybe meditate or go for a walk outside. Whatever works for you.

As long as you understand thoughts vibrate at a certain level and consequently attract similar thoughts to it. You can spiral up or down at your own control depending on what you allow your own thought process to be. Ask anyone who has suffered depression how fast his or her internal dialogue can spiral down into the blackest of places.

Women can be very guilty of this. Have you ever found yourself out to lunch with some friends and everything was fine when you got there but as the conversation goes on and someone starts complaining about her husband, and then the next does too, and before too long all men are evil and you wonder why you are married in the first place? Then, when your partner does come home that afternoon, you are already on the defensive and vibrating at a lower level than usual. How can that possibly help a relationship?

This is the Law of Attraction in operation, and those negative thoughts about men attract more negative thoughts about men, and eventually your relationship gets caught up too. Maybe we should try reminding each other what we really appreciate in our partner and these positive thoughts would benefit the whole group.

As I said before, there are many books on the subject of manifesting and some of them are absolutely fantastic. So, if you wish to get the universe on the same team as you and co-create your reality, then do some homework and check out some of the information out there. I promise you it will be worth it!

CHAPTER 10

THE CONSCIOUS, SUBCONSCIOUS, AND SUPER-CONSCIOUS

Now, keeping all we have discussed in mind and understanding that your own belief system plays a huge role, I would like to move on to some of the more intricate details of living within the Natural Laws.

Many people, even though they are actively participating in manifesting in their life and working in step with the Universe, often find that some really bad stuff (or what they judge to be bad) still happens.

There are several reasons for this. The first has to do with conscious versus sub-conscious versus super-conscious. Wow, that sounds scary! It is a bit to start with. This is where you have to do some work in this co-creation exercise.

You have chosen to come to this reality to experience relativity. By doing so, you are creating preferences and fine tuning those preferences into desires, and of course the universe is answering them. But what you have to understand is you are doing this on three different levels. This is the reason why manifesting is not as easy as simply deciding you want a new Ferrari.

1. **The conscious level**. This is the level where you make decisions. You may be deciding, as you read this book, "That makes sense. I am going to actively participate in the co-creation of my own reality, and the first thing I want is a new car."

2. **The subconscious level**. This is an altogether different matter. It takes a good, honest look in the mirror to really identify what you are manifesting on a subconscious level. What could you possibly be saying on a subconscious level? This is where the hard work is. I only call it hard work because this is the area most people avoid. You really need to do some soul searching, because in most cases this is where the majority of what you have brought into your life so far is coming from. This is almost auto-manifesting. It is in the subconscious that the fear of money exists, the doubt about your worthiness, the concept of greed, the fear of success, and all those other horrible little fears reside. We have collected these fears and assumptions over the years, especially in our childhood. We are often not aware of how many of our parents' fears and attitudes were passed down subconsciously.

3. **The super-conscious level**. This is the mother of all levels, because the truth is, it is very difficult to know what your soul is planning along the way. I often refer to the super-conscious as my "higher self." It is at this level that a lot of life's biggest challenges come, and it is also where you often find the feeling of "fate" rather than free will. As I have said, it is difficult to know, but it is something you can work on with practiced meditation. Meditation helps you to get in touch with your higher self. After several years I have come to the conclusion that I trust my higher self and the experiences it may wish to take part in. There is nothing more frustrating than thinking you are manifesting a certain plan, only to have it turned around 180 degrees on you. However, experience has shown me that the universe, and my super-conscious, knows me better than I know myself, and in all cases, I have ended up with an outcome that I am far happier with.

The bottom line is this: we can control our conscious manifestations relatively easily by watching what we think and say and working towards a positive vibration that attracts what we want. It takes a bit more effort to understand what our subconscious is manifesting, and you will have to trust what your super-conscious is manifesting.

You also need to consider that when something like money comes into your life, it has a flow on effect. Rarely are you the only one whose life is changed, especially in a family situation. When observing your own situation, look particularly at areas of control, especially if it is wealth or relationships you are manifesting. I say this because when we are short of money there are many things that not only we but also our children and spouses cannot afford to do. If you were suddenly wealthy, what freedoms would that give them, and how would you feel about that loss of control?

Sometimes we say we are not happy with a relationship, but when you look deep into it, we are in a place of control, and to change that could mean a loss of control. So as much as you may think you want change, your subconscious could be saying the exact opposite.

Another area that you may want to look at is your subconscious reaction to other people's opinion of you being wealthy or successful or whatever it is you are after. Sadly, in this country, instead of encouraging each other to achieve our personal goals, we tend to take the fearful approach and actually try to cut people down and undermine their efforts. I am sure you have had friends who have laughed and said, "You can't do that" when you were inspired and came up with a good idea. After years, these attitudes sink deep into our subconscious, and we are hesitant to pull away from the mob. This is why our own belief system about wealth is so important. It is stored in the subconscious and affects everything we manifest.

One of the golden rules of understanding the universe and working with it to co-create your own reality is detaching from the good opinion of all people. If you are going to take on other people's negative ideas of what you can and cannot do, you are doomed to failure before you even start.

Don't let anyone hold you back. It is not a secure place to be.

What is security anyway? How can anyone on this planet claim security when we are all sitting on a big rock hurtling through space at some phenomenal speed with heaps of space junk coming the other way? Get real! The only security in this world exists inside you. The security comes from the knowledge that you are an exceptional being who cannot be extinguished, and you have chosen to come here by your own free will. The rest is just an illusion.

As for the super-conscious, as I said earlier, the only way to handle the super-conscious is by trusting that your "higher self" knows exactly what is best for you. You need to stay flexible. Don't be too quick to jump to conclusions. What may appear as bad initially could turn out great. I look back now at past failures and clearly see that the universe was changing my direction. I can honestly say, despite the pain associated with the changes, my family and I always seem to end up in a better place. I am repeatedly surprised how better a situation can become. I am wrong so often when I declare I think I know what I want. This is why sometimes negative situations can turn out to be "get out of jail free" cards. Our super-conscious knows us better than we know ourselves.

The most important thing to remember about the super-conscious is that it is attached to the universal force. The super-conscious is the one part of you that always, always comes from a place of love. It is the super-conscious that makes men run into burning buildings to save complete strangers. It is the super-conscious that comes from a place of forgiveness and peace. It is the voice that gives you a conscious. The super-conscious will never urge you to harm anyone or anything. Negative urges always come from the subconscious, where our fears and prejudices live.

So, manifest to your heart's content, but please remember to take into account the subconscious and the super conscious too, or you will be frustrated with the results.

Also, keep in mind that this same process is happening for every other man, woman, and child on the planet. It is an extremely intricate process, and the very comprehension of how every single event and thought impacts every other soul is where the humility and awe I feel for the universe comes from.

Now, let's move on to some of the other challenges.

CHAPTER 11

TRUST THE UNIVERSAL FORCE

I am going to come back to the Ferrari now, but as I said before, all these points apply whether you are looking for love, trying to improve your marriage, working towards a successful career path—whatever it is.

The area I specifically want to discuss is connected to the subconscious. When we decide we want something, we need to look behind the desire to see what is fuelling it.

In regards to the Ferrari, there are several reasons why one would want a Ferrari. Ironically the easiest one to manifest is not the most common one, i.e., it is a beautiful piece of machinery. If that were honestly, truthfully, and simplistically the only reason you would want one, then it would be easier to bring into your reality than one would expect.

You see, a Ferrari is not just a Ferrari. Besides being an excellent car, the manufacture, by design, has made it a status symbol. This is easily achieved by the price tag. So, when someone owns a Ferrari it says something about that person. It implies success, wealth, position and authority; even if that is not the truth of the situation that is society's implication. The simple truth is that if Ferraris were cheap as chips and everyone drove one, then a huge amount of the attraction would be lost. This is evident upon speaking to locals from the town where Ferraris are built, and they are not so impressed. They desire other types of vehicles, simply because they are over Ferraris. This has to do with the Law of Diminishing Return, which we will be getting to shortly.

The point here is that when you desire a Ferrari for all the normal reasons most would, you do not only desire the car, but you desire to be the sort of person who would own one of those cars. This is really important to understand. The universe is very adept at understanding your desires, and if your desire is to be the sort of person who would own a Ferrari, guess what? You are going to see some major changes, including challenges, in your life to make you the type of person who owns a Ferrari, well before you actually see the car itself.

Further to that, you may be led towards a career that can actually support the car in the first place, because after all, it is not just about buying the car; there are running costs, repairs, maintenance, etc., and of course all parts are expensive in comparison to other vehicles. I imagine the insurance bill alone would be pretty hefty. The universe will take this all into consideration simply because subconsciously you know this to be true—and remember, you are the co-creator!

The point is to trust the universe. Put out what you are after. Be *sure* that you really want it. Be sure of the reasons why you want it. Remember also that the feeling you are ultimately after from that desire can be brought to you a number of different ways. If the only reason you wanted the Ferrari was for the speed and status, you might find yourself with a Lamborghini instead. Stay open-minded and observe.

Work on the subconscious fears, which may be pulling the opposite way. Eliminate as much as possible all negative speak from your life, and then relax and go with the flow.

It is important to understand as well that you should not push too hard against anything that comes your way. The harder you push against the situation, the more of it you will receive in your life, because you are giving the situation so much concentrated thought. Just relax and trust that it is in your life for a reason. When you see a situation occur that you are not comfortable with, think, "That's interesting," as opposed to, "That's bad." Observe rather than judge. Remember, it could be satisfying some subconscious desire, or it could be leading to something else.

Finally, on the subject of super-conscious manifesting, there is one more point that is crucial to understand. All humans need a challenge.

Whether we want to admit that or not is irrelevant. It is the Law of Relativity. Those that overcome the most experience the greatest glory. It is why people climb Mount Everest or explore the jungles of the world. The greatest glory comes from situations that are not easy. Don't expect your journey in life to be easy, because it won't be, and the truth is you don't want it to be. One of the reasons humans are so dramatic in the first place about all sorts of irrelevant crap is because they don't have anything else to be dramatic about, and we all need some challenges or drama in our life. After all, that is what we came here to experience, the relativity of it all.

Ask any person who has just lost a loved one or has a sick child what they think of who won *Australian Idol* that week or what their neighbours are doing.

Humans need something to overcome, something to keep us engaged with the process, something we can match our skills and understanding against. The whole purpose of relativity is to define oneself. If you take all the relativity out of the situation, then you have a problem.

I Wish You Enough

I wish you enough sun to keep your attitude bright.
I wish you enough rain to appreciate the sun more.
I wish you enough happiness to keep your spirit alive.
I wish you enough pain so that the smallest joys in life
appear much bigger.
I wish you enough gain to satisfy your wanting.
I wish you enough loss to appreciate all that you possess.
I wish you enough hellos to get you through
the final good-bye.

So, make your own dramas, and make them real and big. You could try solving world hunger or helping the homeless. You could work towards understanding the human mind and how the universe works or help stamp out the sexual, physical, and mental abuse of children. Climb a mountain, train for the marathon, or go back to university for a degree. With large goals to overcome, you will not have time to complain about your neighbours, and neither will you want to.

The last thing you want to expect from manifesting is a challenge free life, because that is not what life is about. Without the challenges, we would never experience the highs of success, whatever that success means to you. Trust that your super-conscious knows this. In fact, it is highly likely your super-conscious is manifesting a larger purpose for you. It is very unlikely to be a Ferrari. It is far more likely your higher self wants to start an orphanage or something similar. It always comes from a place of serving humanity, so listen to the voice, because happiness is always found in doing what your higher self wants to do.

The universe is an incredibly powerful entity. The same energy that looks after all the living creatures on this planet is capable of looking after us and our seven billion plus spirit friends who came here with us as well.

Your job is to put forward the right thoughts and trust the universe to pull the rest together for you.

CHAPTER 12

THE LAW OF
DIMINISHING RETURN

This brings us to the Law of Diminishing Return. I have already touched on this law briefly several times. It is an extremely important part of the equation.

We have the Law of Relativity, which is basically the reason we are here. It gives us experiences that lead to preferences and on to desires.

Via the Law of Attraction, the universe delivers those sharpest conscious, subconscious, and super-conscious desires to us.

Now, the Law of Diminishing Return guarantees that once we receive our desires, we will "bore" of them and want more or different desires.

Once again I will use the example of chocolate. I love chocolate, seriously love it. If I haven't eaten some for a while, the first chocolate bar is heaven. The second is pretty cool too. Maybe even the third (I said I love chocolate!). But by the fourth, whether I am full or not, the desire is diminishing rapidly. In fact, a fifth one and I would truly be sick.

This, the Law of Diminishing Return, is probably at the cause of the mental health issues that beset people with "perfect" lives. Not only are they feeling uninspired by the lack of challenge in their life, but they are riddled with guilt because they are bored of what they have, even though it appears to be perfect.

When you understand the ramifications of this natural law, you will want to just step back for a moment and reassess the situation.

Just because you are going to get what you want doesn't mean you will stay happy. Will you be happy for a while? Yes, but will the object of your desire continue to deliver the same sense of peace and happiness, day after day, year after year? No, it will not.

Never was there a truer example of the Law of Diminishing Return than a marriage that has gone stale. How could such joy and excitement that existed in the early days of courtship turn to such a state that a couple, once so much in love, speak to each other worse than they would speak to their neighbours or a stranger. Hence the saying "Absence makes the heart grow fonder," or in some cases "Can you just get out of my face for a minute please?" This can be lovers, friends, children, workmates, the dog, the boss—it doesn't matter. We don't take well to too much of a good thing. The Law of Diminishing Return pretty well guarantees that. Hence, the process of preferences and then new desires starts all over again, and hence, the universe continues to expand and you continue to experience new things.

So, as you are pushing forward day after day to get somewhere just take a moment to realise that the finishing line will never appear. You will change your desires and your goals so many times along the way. It is best just to relax on the journey, because that is all you have.

Just the journey.

Even if you made it to retirement lying on the beach, what would you do after the first year? Probably try and buy the little café on the beach and now the challenges start all over again.

Once I fully understood that I would probably never be satisfied then I was able to step back and appreciate what I already had a bit more.

Take a deep breath and relax. After all, we are only here for the experience. It is unlikely we will beat the Law of Diminishing Return. I'm not saying it can't be done. I am sure there are several dedicated monks who have done just that, probably the same monks that have disowned all earthly goods. I am not one of those people, and most of you are not either.

You don't have to look further than the television to see what happens to people who have got the lot, so to speak. An interview with Nicole Richie summed it up when she said, "The problem with having so much money is you get to do just about anything you want, but then you run out of things to exhilarate you."

It is so true!

An example that comes to mind was an interview with the founder of a famous Australian surf brand who, when asked about his recent new business venture, reluctantly admitted that even though he was very cashed up and the business had virtually 100 per cent chance of success, it was nowhere near the excitement of the early days when he first started his surf line. This is where he had challenges, close calls, and cash was tight. The sense of achievement and pride was much stronger then.

So, have your desires and put them out there, but find the faith, both in yourself as an eternal soul and in the co-operation of the universe, to let things unfold as they do. That is, without judgement of what is supposed to be good or bad.

Trust that what is put before you, no matter how tempted you are to call it bad, will in some obscure way end up turning out the best for you and those you love. And most important of all, enjoy the small successes along the way.

CHAPTER 13

FREE WILL VERSUS FATE?

Now, before we get onto a few of the finer challenges, I would like to take a moment to discuss free will versus fate.

Observation has shown me that to successfully run a universe of over 7 billion souls while constantly monitoring every preference and desire expressed by every single one of those souls requires some serious manipulation by the powers that be. Coincidences are so much more than what could otherwise appear to be random meetings or situations.

Once I started observing myself closely, I noticed strange little things happening like; one minute I would be in the shower, deep in thought, and the next I would be standing out on the mat drying myself. Sometimes, I would think, "Hey, what am I doing here? I wasn't ready to get out yet." I have learnt to accept that someone must think I am running behind schedule.

I figure it is the same for lost car keys, missing wallets and handbags, red lights, slow drivers, and any of the things that slow you down some days. Don't get mad. See the situations for what they are. Road rage is so silly. There is probably a reason you are being held up. The universe is simply adjusting your schedule. If there are people you are meant to meet and places you are meant to be at, at a certain time (God's time, not your time), then it stands to reason that the universe will use ways and means of adjusting your timetable. Don't get mad in traffic; thank the universe for intervening instead.

So, if coincidences are real, and the universe is busy organising people, places, and things, then where does our control come in?

Firstly, we have the free will to decide to come here in the first place. Then we have the free will to make preferences and therefore desires. It is from that point that the universe takes over and finds ways to make those desires come to you. The universe handles the nuts and bolts of the situation, so therefore it stands to reason that fate plays a large role on a day-to-day basis, and free will is the ability to control the thoughts in the first place. Don't forget, at any given time the universe is working with more than 7 billion people on this planet alone. You get what you think about. Use your free will to control the thoughts and then fate will deliver them to you.

When it comes to death, again we can manifest our own death from one of any of the three levels: conscious, subconscious, or super-conscious The first thing we need to comprehend here is that there is nothing scary about death.

Death is your right. In fact, I don't even like the word death, because nobody actually dies. I like to think of it more like becoming invisible. People don't die; they just become invisible to those of us still here in this reality of relativity. This transition is every person's right. For goodness' sake, who would want to hang around here in the land of relativity forever? The least we are entitled to is a rest and a holiday every now and then, even if we do decide to come back again. I will grant you there are some scary ways to die, but like all relativity, anything you can imagine is available, even a zillion different ways to die. Just listen to the news. Maybe the news should be retitled "Interesting ways people have chosen to go home today." The options are endless.

From my observation of life, I have no choice but to determine that the time of your death, or anyone else's for that matter, is decided before we come here. It is decided on a super-conscious level. I think we must all set our date before we come. Something akin to buying the return airfare upfront. We want to make sure we are going to get home. I have seen so many instances in my life where people have experienced such tragic circumstances and survived, and yet other people have died by being hit by a sign walking down the street or something equally random. The bottom line is we all have the right to go home, and we already know when and how that will be.

There is an argument, however, to suggest that in certain circumstances people can take themselves home early, either via conscious suicide or more on a subconscious level. It is not uncommon for a spouse when they lose their partner of many, many years to follow them to the grave within the year. It is also noted by some oncologists that occasionally some patients almost seem to be relieved to be diagnosed with cancer. They feel their lives are so hopeless, or they feel they are drowning in responsibility and there is no honourable way out of the situation without letting their loved ones down.

In addition, I have also heard numerous accounts of people, having just reached retirement, suddenly dying. I consider this subconscious suicide, driven by the lack of challenge or the loss of relevance. I think there are some extreme sports people who could be guilty of subconscious suicide too.

Then, of course, there is conscious suicide. Once again, the soul has the right to go home anytime it likes. The sad part is that once they get back to the other side I am sure they would regret bailing out and would want to come back again. Life is an eternal gift. It is an honour to come into this world. To give up on it is something that I am sure, we would truly regret when we returned home.

Before going any further I would like to clarify my beliefs as to why people get cancer or other life-threatening illnesses. It is not as easy as saying, "Well, you manifested it into your own reality."

Keeping in mind that we are manifesting on three levels at all times, the disease could be coming from any one of those three levels. It is true that, on a conscious level, you could have brought it into your life by putting your attention on the disease constantly. You should never focus too much attention on illness of any nature, whether that is through television, reading, or simply talking with other people.

Then, as I just mentioned, there are those that Deepak Chopra and others have identified who probably brought the disease in on a subconscious level, because they truly have had enough of this reality and they are tired and just want to go home. This only the patient will truly know himself, and it is very unlikely he will ever want to admit it to someone else, because society doesn't accept us wanting to die early, for any reason. Society dictates that we should all want to stay on this earth for as long as possible, and any choice other than that is deemed an act of selfishness.

On a subconscious level, there is also the situation where the medical profession has diagnosed a fatal disease, and because we put so much faith in the medical establishment, we believe them and their timeframes, even if they are not correct. Sadly, we can bring our death forward, just because we believe on a subconscious level that they could not possibly be wrong.

Then again, there is the super-conscious level. This is where the higher self has chosen the disease to, firstly, give the patient the experience but also to provide a situation that allows their loved ones to experience compassion, empathy, and potentially loss while they are on their journey. You would have decided this experience before you ever came into this world.

Finally, there is the disease we get that we eventually recover from, which often has far-reaching ramifications in our lives. It is not uncommon to meet survivors of cancer who can identify positive life changes that came about because of their disease. These may be changes in situations that they were strongly manifesting, and the disease is simply the catalyst that bought about that change.

Again, we have to be careful not to judge. If you are suffering from a life-threatening illness, only you can truly know in your heart which level you feel the disease is coming from. No doctor, no therapist, no loved one can do that for you, and as a loved one of the person with the disease, we have no right to judge how they handle the situation, because we can never truly know.

It is interesting to speak to people, or read about people, who have had a near death experience. It is often commented that your life does flash before your eyes in the moment of your death; however, as referred to at the end of the movie *American Beauty*, those seconds can seem to stretch out into an "ocean of time." It is not the major dramas of our lives that we remember during this time, either; it is the small and somewhat insignificant things that we take for granted on a day to day basis, like a cool summer breeze or a beautiful moon rising. It is not the pain or anxiety that makes up the pattern of our life but rather the loving touch of a child or a smile from a friend.

Our lives, and the dramas we create within our reality, seem to be so important to us at the time, and we can often feel like we are drowning. Many who contemplate suicide often comment that they just want the pain to stop. We need to remember somehow, amongst the pain, that we came here to experience these feelings and how unimportant, in the big picture, are the events and people that are causing the pain. It is important to remember that it is the insignificant little things in life that we will remember, and it is these same little insignificant events that we will feel an overwhelming gratitude for, in our last days in this reality. It will be those minor day-to-day events that we will be so honoured to have experienced, and the rest of the pain and suffering that we may have gone through will be left behind to wash away in the "ocean of time."

It is sometimes hard to understand that your life is both as insignificant as it is grand and that when it is over you will be incredibly grateful for the "simple little life" you had.

Life is such an honour. Such a gift! It is far too precious a gift to give up on. When, on those rare occasions we feel the universal force flow through us, it is in these moments that we can truly feel the gratitude for this simple but valuable gift called life. We should honour every day that we have the privilege of participating in this world of relativity.

And don't forget, the only judgement any of us will have to endure when we return home is our own judgement.

At the end of the day, the mind is a very powerful tool, and as much as you can manifest many things into your life, you can also manifest yourself home. So even in death we have free will, if we want to use it. If we don't, then there is obviously a predetermined time to go as well. The bottom line is we all go home, and instead of viewing it as sadness, consider it as your graduation ceremony. Whatever you came here to do, have, experience, or achieve has been accomplished.

Does that mean we won't leave in the middle of something? Of course we will! I hope I will! As I said before, there is no finishing line. Most of us will leave this vibrational plane in the middle of trying to achieve something, but that's okay. That is the way it is meant to be. Some of us will leave at a very young age, having only come here for a short time. Others hang around for over a century. At the end of the day, it doesn't matter. We came here to experience, and whether we experience for ten years or one hundred years, we have done what we came here to do and we have affected a whole lot of other souls along the way. Sometimes some of the younger ones leave the most lasting impressions. Life isn't measured in years; it is measured in experiences and how you affect the experiences of the people around you while you are here.

Finally, on the subject of free will versus fate, I want to discuss a point that often comes up when discussing the power of deliberate intent and manifesting, and that is how much of this is your effort. If you work harder, will it happen faster? If you push harder, will that make it more likely?

The answer is that it is more important to be observant than actually take decisive action. Through observation you will gain a better understanding of whether it is the right time to take action or relax and go with inaction. In fact, sometimes we could be pulling against what the universe is trying to bring us.

Sure, you may have to take some action to make things happen, but it is more important that you be observant. In fact, not taking action can sometimes be harder than actually trying to make it happen and sometimes inaction is exactly what is called for.

Again, trust the universe that your thoughts on a conscious, subconscious, and super-conscious level are being brought to you at all times. Look for the clues and work with the universe to make it happen.

You have the free will to put out into the universe whatever it is you desire by your thoughts and words. Fate is the universe bringing those desires to you.

CHAPTER 14

DEALING WITH PEOPLE

Now I want to touch on some of the finer challenges you will have along the way.

The first one is people. When you start hearing how often people are speaking negatively in your environment, I think you will be as amazed. I think this problem may be worse in Australia than other countries, because we have a tendency to bond in the negative. A cheerful person on a Monday morning is rarely greeted warmly!

When I first understood the importance of the types of conversations I was having, it became apparent that many people in my life were either negative or untrustworthy. I noticed for the first time how much gossip and negative talk I participated in on a daily basis. I remember feeling a bit overwhelmed with all the negativity. I meditated on this situation and asked my guides (which we all have, remember) to help me out. I simply said, "Could you please help me by taking all the seriously negative and untrustworthy people out of my life. I only wish to be close to people who are positive influences in my life."

Well, again, be careful what you ask for. Over the coming weeks and months, I started seeing all sorts of people being untrustworthy, false, and surprisingly negative. One by one they disappeared from my life. I experienced conflict with people I never thought I would. I made a conscious decision to remove them from my life and just stopped seeing them and others just fell away for their own reasons.

These days I have a much smaller circle of friends, but they are people who are trustworthy, positive people and that works for me.

I won't for one minute tell you that it was easy. A lot of people will try and guilt trip you into many things. Observe your relationships and see for yourself how much you are involved in certain situations because of guilt, or which people you bond with by gossiping or complaining about life or other people. Try and remove as many of the negative people from your life, or talk to them and explain that you are not interested in a relationship based in negativity anymore. Keep in mind they probably won't like it. Believe in yourself and march forward anyway. It's your life and it's up to you what you want your reality to be.

Remember, detach from the good opinion of all people.

Run your own race.

Another area where it can get sticky with people is when they want to discuss health issues for long periods of time.

I will not sit and discuss the negative aspects of someone's health in great detail any more than I will recount all the negative health issues I have had. I am truly pained when loved ones or friends are worried about an illness; however, using all the powers of the universe, I behave in a way that assumes their healing. I tell them how strong they are and talk about the healthy things that are working fine. I am not discounting their fear. If it is serious, I will acknowledge that, but I act to counteract their illness. I can't do anything to help if I am thinking thoughts of doom and gloom and vibrating on a level that will attract more thoughts of doom and gloom. Ever noticed how hypochondriacs are the sickest people you know?

Obviously, when it comes to serious illness, it is easier said than done, but on the day-to-day issues, such as sore backs, knees, flus, colds, headaches, and so on, don't say anything. The more times you confirm the flu the longer you will have it. I rarely get sick anymore. I can't actually remember the last time I was sick. However, I do have a back that seems to be directly linked to how much money is in the bank, which I find quite amusing. As soon as I am feeling financially crippled, my back responds in kind. Talk about manifesting from the subconscious.

If you or someone you know does have serious health issues, then I would recommend readings by Dr. Deepak Chopra and Louise Hay. They both have very powerful messages in the areas of healing. Deepak, as I mentioned, is an oncologist, and Louise Hay has written multiple books on healing with the mind. Louise Hay has also had to deal with the experience of Cancer herself. If healing and health is an area of concern to you, a search of any decent bookshop will produce some fine literature on the subject.

Finally, on the subject of people, at the end of the day the Law of Attraction will determine who is in your life anyway. When you become calmer and more at peace with your current situation, you will begin to vibrate higher than you currently do. And as you make changes in your life that bring about a higher and higher vibration level you may have difficulties with people that you once got along with really well. The physical reason is simply that you are not vibrating at a compatible level with them anymore. This would be one reason why so many people "grow apart." It is not so much that they like golf and you like movies. It is that you are actually vibrating at two different levels, and vibration is like water—it finds its own level.

On a good note, though: you will also attract more people into your life that vibrate at your new higher level. In fact, people that may have irritated you before may feel more comfortable now.

Keep in mind this unfortunately does work in the reverse too. The lower you vibrate, the more you will attract angrier, negative people into your life.

The point I wanted to make is that, ultimately, you are going to have to decide how you handle the traditional habits of society, such as sitting around talking about being sick, especially in the older population. You will also have to deal with people who always have negative conversations about relationships or lack of money and numerous other perceived hardships. Personally, I just walk away and refuse to discuss subjects that revolve around sickness or negativity in any area.

Your imagination is a very powerful tool, and the universe listens. Don't participate in imagining scenarios that you would consider negative, and don't get into conversations with other people about those scenarios either, or you will help bring them or a similar situation into your life.

Now, I would like to go on to some day-to-day things that will make it easier for you to actively co-create, with the universe, to see the reality you would like to see. But before we do, let's recap.

- You are an eternal soul who normally resides in heaven. You are not a human having a spiritual experience; you are a spirit having a human experience.

- The only reason you are here is to experience relativity. If you do nothing more than that, and then return home, you have achieved all that you set out to do. You are a human just being!

- The universe, your guides and countless angels unconditionally love you and are there to help you wherever possible. All you have to do is ask.

- There is nothing to prove and there is nothing to be earned. We all go home.

- Through your experiences you will create preferences which, when sharpened, become your desires.

- The universe brings to you all your sharpest desires on a conscious, subconscious, and super-conscious level through the Law of Attraction.

- The Law of Diminishing Return guarantees that you will continually change your preferences and desires.

- It is through you overcoming your own challenges that your greatest pride is felt; hence, you further define yourself and who you are.

- It is virtually impossible for you to understand what is good or bad for you, at any given point in time, because the Law of Relativity, the Law of Attraction and the Law of Diminishing Return are operating on a conscious, subconscious, and super-conscious level at all times.

- The universe answers what you put out through your thoughts, words and actions; every time without fail!

- Trust that the universe and your higher self understand what you need better than you do, but participate in the process of co-creating your reality everyday.

- Free will gives you the ability to put your preference and desires forward; however, fate takes a hand in bringing those desires to you.

CHAPTER 15

Now Time and Meditation

So, how do you do this on a daily basis?

Firstly, relax and know it is all a game. I can't say it enough. You are only here to experience relativity, so an experience is an experience no matter what you are doing.

Secondly, meditate every day. Meditation is your most direct route to understanding not only your subconscious and super-conscious desires but it is also the tool you need to communicate with the universe. The stronger connection you have with the universe and your higher self (super-conscious), the more effectively you will be able to manifest the "perfect" life for yourself.

There are many types of meditation. One of the most important types of meditation is what I call "Now Time." It is finding the quiet space in your mind where you can hear the universe. Does this mean you have to completely quiet your mind and have no thoughts? No, it does not. In fact, this type of meditation can come in the form of running, painting, listening to music, sitting and concentrating on your breathing, or swimming. Meditation is the ability to slow your mind down and keep it in the "now" instead of thinking about the past or what could happen in the future. Observe your own thoughts and you will find that thoughts about the past or the future occupy our minds 95 per cent of the time. We need some "Now Time."

Start out with maybe only five minutes a day, and gradually build that up. You will find that it will be something you will enjoy. It is quite tiring and draining worrying about the past or the future every second of the day. When you get use to times when your brain slows down and stays in the now, you will find it really relaxing and refreshing. If you want to read something really cool about being in the Now, Eckhart Tolle's *The Power of Now* and *Stillness Speaks* are great books to start with. Better still; listen to the audio books, which are so soothing. You can buy these directly from ITunes, Audible and the like. Many of them are also still available on CD.

As I said, you do not have to stop to do this form of meditating. You can have Now Time just washing the dishes. Instead of washing dishes while your brain wanders off fretting about the past or worrying about the future, turn your attention to the now and see how warm the water feels on your hands. Be grateful for the fact you have dishes to wash in the first place. Check out the pattern on your plates. Don't form any opinions, just observe. Look out the window in front of you and really notice the plants instead of just staring with that glazed expression of someone deep in thought. You can do this with gardening or mowing the lawn. In fact, I have heard your plants will grow better if you concentrate on them when you are gardening. Even if you are driving, actually pay attention to driving. How long has it been since you were a teenager and driving was something you did just because you loved the physical act of driving? Think about the steering wheel under your fingers, your foot on the pedal, and the size of the vehicle you are controlling.

You can use so many experiences in a day to be in the Now. Probably the most important one is when your kids or spouse are talking to you. Take a moment to stop and really look at them. Be in the now with them, not thinking of something else so you only half hear what they are saying, or worse still, thinking about what you are going to reply before they have even finished speaking.

Actually, if you do this with most people you meet, you will find yourself getting a lot more cooperation. People like being really listened to. They like knowing they have you "in the now," listening to them instead of planning what you are going to say next or worrying about next week's meeting.

Many successful people have said in the past that their best inspirational thoughts came to them while they were in the Now. It is during this quiet time of the mind that the universe can get through to you the easiest.

Then there is the sit-down-type mediation.

Again, start with only a small amount of time per day, say fifteen minutes In the morning and another fifteen minutes at night. You will find there are heaps of books available on how to meditate, but I will run you through a quick description of what I do when I meditate. Like all areas of this subject, there are as many suggestions as there are readers.

Personally, I break my meditation into five different exercises of only a couple of minutes each. I would like to add that it is helpful if you meditate in the same place every day—maybe an armchair in your bedroom or a quiet place outside. The reason it is good to meditate in the same place is that your body, quite quickly actually, will begin to recognise the initial steps to meditating, and it will automatically begin to get you in the frame of mind you are after as soon as you sit down and close your eyes.

The first thing I do when I am comfortable is relax. It sounds so simple, yet we spend so much of our day in a state of tension. Start with your head and work down your body, letting the tension and stress drain away. Imagine you are a dead weight and feel your body falling into the chair. Pay attention to your breathing and aim to slow it down to a nice, steady pace. As you do this your thoughts will slow down too, and as I said, the more often you do this, especially if you do it in the same place each time, the more quickly your body will begin to relax and slow down.

In really stressful times I have been known to "shhh" myself and add a slight rock (much as one would a baby) to help the mind to slow down and relax.

Next, after I feel quite relaxed, I start to observe the feelings and noises around me. This is where I mentally remind myself that I am a spirit having a human experience.

I pretend I come from a place of no past and no future. It is only me, here now, in this chair, and nothing else exists for this brief period of time. That can actually be a remarkable feeling in itself. I then use all my senses—hearing, feeling, tasting, smell, and sight (in my mind's eye)—to pick up any indications that I have my guides and the universal force around me.

I picture them hovering around and I mentally use the space where the third eye is supposed to be (in the middle of your forehead) to put out a radio-like signal to see what comes back. The theory here is the more you look, listen, and feel for your guides the stronger, the connection becomes and over time they will find a way to get through to you. At some stage a few people may start to see images in their mind's eye, while others may hear or feel ideas and thoughts. This is extremely personal, as it is so different for everyone. The whole idea is simply to be still and observe while being aware they are there and trying to communicate to you.

Next, start thinking of all the things you are grateful for. Think of it as your time to report back to "head office." Run through the things in your mind that you are grateful for, and literally there are hundreds when you get thinking about them. If you are finding it difficult to be grateful, think of this saying: "I was sad I had no shoes until I met the man who had no feet. Then I was just grateful I had feet."

Thank your guides, and the universe, for the many small things you may have experienced recently that you can attribute to them. This begins to raise your vibration level further. All the time, remember to be aware of what you are feeling, hearing, and seeing in your mind's eye.

Finally, I move from gratitude to visualisation. I start to think of how I will feel when I do get such and such, whatever it is I am after. For example, if you are after healing, picture yourself vibrant and healthy skipping around a park or participating in a triathlon—whatever does it for you. What you are actually after is the feeling that achieving that goal would bring you. Stay completely detached from the outcome. You are only "guessing" you want to achieve that goal, because the universe may be aware you are really on a completely different track, which you will understand yourself in the near future.

Again, going back to the Ferrari, how would you feel when you had it? Focus on that feeling of joy and pride. As I mentioned before, the universe may actually bring you a Lamborghini instead, because it generates the exact same feelings. Either way it is the feeling you want to focus on. If it's a money situation you want to fix, how would you feel when it was resolved? Focus on that sense of relief.

It is the feeling that is actually vibrating, and that is what the universe will set about to bring you—more of that great feeling.

The last thing you need to do is just relax for a couple minutes and focus on how much the divine universe loves you and every single little thing you do. Just feel that love for a minute or two. It will carry with you throughout the day.

So, that is my basic meditation:

1. Relax.
2. Send out energy to your guides and the universe and observe what you feel, hear, see, taste, and smell.
3. Run through many things that you are grateful for, especially those things which may have happened since last time you mediated.
4. Visualise the feelings you are trying to manifest to yourself.
5. Finally, just for the smallest amount of time, try to think nothing except that a divine universe loves you and this truth will never change. Try to feel this love and peace in your heart rather than think about it.

During your meditation, note any ideas or thoughts that come out of the blue, as these are often the answers to the challenges that are confronting you at the time.

The longer you practice meditating and observing yourself and others, the more you see in every situation. I have heard of people who, after meditating for a year or so, started Astral travelling in their meditations. Others started seeing visions as answers to their questions. Some feel the answers stronger and stronger the longer they practice. Everyone is different, but everyone has his or her personal connection to the universe.

Stick with it and you will find your own connection. Do whatever works for you; just build that connection.

Meditating is the glue that holds the whole lot together. It gives you the space to quiet the mind and remember that this reality is an illusion. It gives you a chance to get it all back in perspective again before you reach back out into the world of relativity. It gives you an opportunity to mentally be aware of those around you that you cannot see but are with you at all times and to strengthen that connection.

Above all, meditating allows a moment of peace in a world that bombards us with so much information and so many opinions. It gives the mind a place to be quiet, even if it is only for a short period.

Now, I would like to move on to one of the hardest parts; knowing yourself.

CHAPTER 16

KNOWING AND OBSERVING

To really know yourself you need to take an honest look at what your subconscious fears and prejudices may be. What are you gaining by the negative dramas in your life? As Dr. Phil says, there is a payout for all the negative experiences we stay with. I believe this to be true. You will manifest what you need. What could you be gaining by having a certain drama or negativity in your life? You invited it there, so why and how can you approach it from a different angle? One of the most interesting points in the DVD *What the Bleep Do We Know* is the concept that the body actually becomes addicted to the different chemicals produced by our emotions. In other words, naturally angry people are actually addicted, as one would be with heroin, to the chemical that is produced when one is angry. That is an interesting thought in itself. What emotions are you experiencing in large amounts every day?

If you can determine that you are not bringing negativity into your life on a conscious level, and then you can also

truly and honestly say you don't think you are doing it on a subconscious level, then you will have to make the assumption that whatever is coming in to your life is coming from your super-conscious, in which case, relax on it, because it must be for a reason. The trick is to be observant and recognise when you are contributing negativity or fear to the situation.

It is also important to understand that once you have put a desire forward and made sure you are not putting any blocks up to stop it entering your life, you must let go and trust the universe. If you are obsessing over the desire, it just attracts more obsessive feelings and puts out the message that you don't believe you will get it in the end, or you wouldn't be obsessing. Hence, the universe will give you your belief, which is you won't get it. We don't stress about the sun coming up in the morning. We don't have to ask every day for the sun to come up. We just "know" that it will, so we don't need to ask.

Next, become an observer of yourself and the world. This is something Eckhart Tolle talks about a lot. Take the time just to stop, whether it is in a shopping centre or at the traffic lights, and watch the people around you with the understanding that they too are mighty souls who, like you, were brave enough to come here to experience relativity. The more you do this, the more compassion you feel for the human race, especially as you start to calm down and find some peace. It becomes evident how many people are literally riddled with fear in this life. Become an observer of yourself as well. When you are under pressure and start feeling stressed, observe the feelings and try and "step aside" for a moment to understand what your mind and emotions are doing.

A little exercise that helps me in stressful times is to sit in a quiet place, eyes closed, and think to myself, "As I sit here right in this moment there is actually nothing wrong" Now sometimes, particularly in really scary situations, you might only be able to project forward enough to say, "As I sit here now, there is nothing in the next five minutes that is wrong," and in calmer times you may be able to think the whole day is fine. The point is that most of our fears are actually being dragged into our conscious from the future; most of the time they are not actually happening in that exact moment. Find a few seconds in that moment to feel safe. It will help to restore your balance.

There is another excellent little experiment to try. When your mind is flat out thinking about all sorts of negative scenarios, turn on it (so to speak) and say, "What are you going to worry about next?" It is funny how, when you put your attention on your own thought process, the brain often tends to freeze in shyness.

If you practice this art of observing, you will eventually start to understand the way your mind works. You will be able to recognise when it is running away in fear and creating drama simply because it is bored or looking for some form of gratification. Then you will have the ability to redirect those thoughts to ones that are more relaxing and peaceful.

Much can be gained by observing your own actions and behaviours from a calm, relaxed perspective, without judgement.

When manifesting, start small. Make sure it is within your belief system. There is no point saying you want to manifest a million dollars into your life directly if a million dollars is too far out of your belief system. Start with a slightly better car or a slightly better house, or just losing 10 kg. Whatever it is, stay within your belief system. This is why it is important to observe yourself so you can identify what your belief system is.

It is far more beneficial to manifest a smaller thing and then experience the joy of achieving it, because the universe will react to that feeling of joy and bring you more of that. If you make too large a leap, you may feel disappointed, and the universe will react by bringing more disappointment into your life. This is a curly one for people who are struggling under a huge mortgage. Sometimes it may be more productive to downsize, by selling your house, because it takes the stress away and you can stop manifesting more stress.

On that point, if you want to experience living in a certain type of home in a certain place, the universe does not distinguish between renting and buying. It is about the experience, remember? A couple of years ago, I experienced a unit overlooking the ocean with the most stunning views. It was only for six months, and interestingly that was long enough as I concluded I don't like unit living. The point is that it would have cost me over one million dollars to buy that unit. Instead we paid only $400 a week in rent and still achieved the same experience.

Remember that it is experiences that you are trying to collect while you are here, not material possessions. Sometimes owning your own home actually stops you moving around and experiencing new things. Having said that, I believe real estate is the most secure of all investment opportunities. However, you can own houses for financial security and rent them out to other people whilst you rent too. This way you have the flexibility and adaptability to experience many new things whilst still achieving capital gains. This also allows you to live in houses that would perhaps be out of your price range to purchase.

You're here for a good time, not a long time. Get into it and experience as much as you can.

This brings me to the next point. Stop judging people, situations, or circumstances as good or bad. As we have already mentioned, it is most important not to judge, because you seriously can't tell without the hindsight that is only offered by time. Just practice one day at a time. "Today, I will judge nothing as good or bad. I will just experience the situations as they occur."

Finally, in this chapter, recognise that our world still runs on fear, and so do you. The fear of there not being enough, the fear of getting hurt, the fear of being rejected, the fear of hell, the fear of dying, the fear of a loved one dying. There are so many fears that people live with every moment. Recognise these fears in yourself. Try to recognise when your reactions to certain situations may be based in fear.

My opinion is that all people are basically good, but we live with such incredible amounts of fear. I approach all people with a knowing that they are motivated by that fear and as such could turn on me at any time. Even the worst of us were born innocent. It isn't until life and relativity gets to us that the fear and anger grows, obviously with some more than others.

"Morals are the privilege of the affluent." There is some truth to that. As a mother I know I have a certain set of morals I live by in this country, but put me in a different circumstance—for example, where my children were potentially starving—and I could turn to theft as quickly as the next person. Australia was built on convicts who stole. If you were trying to harm my children, under those circumstances, I am sure I would be capable of murder as well.

The point is expect the best from all people and treat them accordingly, again, as you would want to be treated, but be careful too. We are all motivated by fear, and some people draw the line sooner than others when it comes to protecting their own self-interests, especially when it comes to money

CHAPTER 17

EMBRACING CHANGE

One final important issue: dealing with change. This is perhaps the hardest thing to do. Change and uncertainty tend to unravel most of us. Don't be scared of change or uncertainty. Change is the only way the universe can get you from one place to the next, and uncertainty is the best way to leave all potentially positive options open.

I was saddened to hear on the news that Ford in Melbourne will be shutting down its plant in three years. The employees have all been given three years' notice. However, that was not what saddened me. What saddened me was the reaction of some of those workers. They were very angry and hostile about their situation. They perceived themselves as victims who had been harshly treated.

Firstly, it is an economical decision on behalf of Ford, but more importantly, how often does a person get three years' notice that they are going to be fired? Three years surely gives them enough time to plan where they want to go from there.

I wish people could relax and appreciate that if things change, there is a very good chance they are changing for the better. Hanging on to a certain situation with tight, fearful hands will not help you grow and experience all that you can in your life. Take change as an opportunity to experience something different. Give yourself the chance to like something even more.

We live in a completely different society now, and I don't think as a society we have a strong understanding of that change. I am not convinced that people actually understand the implications of the Internet and computers in every home.

Let's look back at history for a moment. Over the centuries the wealth in the world has basically stayed in the same hands the whole way along. If you were born into money you tended to keep it. If you were not born into money it would take a minor miracle to obtain wealth. The primary reason for such a tight class structure was education. Education was the key. Those with money could afford the education, including university. Therefore, those with money graduated university and went on to hold the positions of power. Over the centuries, knowledge, and therefore power, has tended to stay in the hands of people with money.

Ultimately, it is knowledge that holds power, not money. Anyone with the knowledge can make the money.

These days knowledge is available to literally everyone on the planet who can plug a computer in and get on the Internet. This is noticeable even in the family home, where, as a mother, I watch my kid's access information for assignments that would never have been available to them in the past.

One needs to simply have a question come into their mind. Then, by taking a few steps to a computer and a few keystrokes on Google, we can have that question answered for us, whether we are rich or poor, healthy or ill. It doesn't matter.

What this means for society is that the class structure is collapsing, especially in Australia, where it was never as strong in the first place as it was in England. Knowledge is no longer in the hands of the rich; it is now available to all.

Several decades ago, if you wanted to learn about money there was very little information available. Now you could spend a lifetime reading and studying the mountain of material that successful people have put out there for our benefit. There really is every opportunity available to us.

The Internet has also given us the ability to work or to run businesses from home at a fraction of the cost of setting up a traditional retail outlet or manufacturing plant. We don't have to be Henry Ford to make millions of dollars anymore.

The first thing we have to do though is understand the reason we are here in the first place and then let go of the fear of failure.

John C. Maxwell writes one of the best books I have ever read on the subject of business failure, *Failing Forward*. Mr. Maxwell says on the cover of his book, "The difference between average people and achieving people is their perception of and response to failure."

Business and work are no different to the concepts in the *Bhagavad-Gita*, as long as you go into a job or business with an honourable heart and the right intention. If someone loses out financially by your hand, or you by theirs, remember, they chose to play the business game too, and neither of you was really hurt. You both just had an experience. The goal is to learn from that experience and take those lessons with you into the next venture.

Australians have a new opportunity in front of them. We already have a very high rate of entrepreneurship in this country, and I would like to see more encouraged. I think every Australian has the right to own and run his or her own business. Even a labourer on a building site can have a contract labour company.

Whether it is in real estate, the stock market, an online shop, or whatever takes your fancy, it all comes down to letting go of fear and learning to live with change. Fear is the product of relativity. We may have volunteered to come here to experience relativity, but we are capable of controlling, to some degree, how much of that negativity we have to experience.

I can tell you now, the majority of stress humans feel in their life is brought on by letting their minds run away with horrible imaginings of what could go wrong. Ninety per cent of what you imagine can go wrong never does. Then you need to ask the question anyway: what is considered wrong? The only thing I can think that we could be doing wrong is spending so much time stressing over situations that we end up manifesting far more stress, and the cycle continues. Well, I suppose that isn't even wrong, just plain sad. Try to remember, even during darker times, that change always precedes something better.

On a similar point, look after what you already have. Let's say you are after a new car because your current one is getting old and rusty, you should still look after that old car. Don't spend time thinking about what is wrong with it; instead, be grateful for the things on it that work and spend time thinking about the beautiful new car. By taking care of what we already have, no matter how basic those things are, we are giving out feelings of gratitude and letting the universe know that we are prepared for the beautiful new car.

On the same note, don't collect clutter. If you want lots of new things in your life, then make room for them. Get rid of all stuff you simply do not use. Hoarding is often a sign of a subconscious fear of there not being enough. Donate it all to a charity or have a garage sale. Clutter deters us from positively inviting in new stuff, especially if your place is already feeling cluttered.

Change is what life is all about. Society is changing so quickly on a daily basis now. Embrace change. Be excited about change. It comes back to trusting the universe.

Trust that the changes in your life are leading you towards the life you wish to co-create for yourself.

CHAPTER 18

STAYING ON TRACK

Just a final few points. These ideas are random and in no particular order; however, I feel you will benefit from them.

Firstly, believe only your own truth. There are so many ideas and theories about life, the universe, and everything. Only believe what you feel in your heart to be the truth. You will recognise your truth when you hear it, because it seems so logical and natural. Don't let anyone convince you that you need him or her to get to God. That is so untrue and one of the big issues I have with organised religion. We all have a direct link to the universe through our thought processes, and if you take the time to meditate and get to know your own thoughts, you will find a comfortable, easy friendship with your own version of God.

I found it interesting recently when I had the opportunity to attend a Christian church to hear a guest speaker. Before the speaker came on stage, the congregation bowed their heads in prayer. After many years of meditating, I found it rather awkward and stilted repeating words of a standard prayer. I consider myself "in prayer" with the universe all day long via my thoughts, words, and actions. I talk to God and my guides all day, every day. To officially pray felt like knocking on my own front door at home and asking if I could speak to one of my children. We are already in prayer with the universe every moment of every day and during those times when you take a moment to recognise this you are strengthening your connection.

Listen to your mind and body. Often you will have moments of inspiration, intuition, or a general knowing that something is right or wrong for you. One of the signs that you have just read or heard something that is truth for you is the goose bumps, butterflies in your stomach, or hair standing up on the back of your neck. It may also bring tears to your eyes. Pay attention when this happens; it is the universe communicating with you.

I also strongly suggest you read, read, read. There are some fantastic books out there that offer so much insight into this subject. If you can't find the time or a strong inclination to read, then look for the equivalent in CD or DVD form. Most of the world's best sources on this subject are now being released in an audio form.

If one of your goals is to increase your income source or cash flow, I also suggest you start reading books like *Rich Dad, Poor Dad*, by Robert Kiyosaki, and authors like Jamie McIntyre, an Australian. In my experience, it is good to be educated about money when riches start to fall in your lap. One of the most critical parts of the experience is the education. You want to have money? Then you need to get to know money. Get to know as much as you can about it. Take a basic business course or study the stock market. Start frequenting open houses in your area if you are interested in real estate or renovation.

Seek as much independent information as you can so you can be well informed in your decisions. It will also help you to spot opportunity when it does come knocking at your door, and you will be ready and knowledgeable enough to take action.

When reading, don't take one book as gospel. Read as many alternative books on the subject as you can. There are many ways to skin a cat, as they say, and there are many authors with many ideas that you can put into practice to help you achieve what you desire.

Don't be too staunch about your decisions either. The older I get, the more I realise I don't know. I think that could be said for many people. Don't be afraid to say, "Oh, I never thought of that." You are going to change your mind about many things over the years. Have your beliefs, but with humility, not arrogance.

Unlike most people, I believe wealth and spirituality are indeed connected rather than opposite. There is nothing holy in going without in a world of such abundance. It is our responsibility to use this time to be the best we can be at whatever we choose to be involved with. I don't care if you are the garbage collector for the area; be the best garbage collector there is, whilst focusing your positive energy on moving into the career you want to be in or starting a garbage removal company.

Be grateful! Now, I know a lot of books write about gratitude being the key to successful manifesting, and they are right. Not because you are busy thanking the universe for what you have. The universe does not need thanks. It is only doing what it is designed to do. It is providing us with our desires based on what we are putting out. What gratitude does, and the reason it works, is that when you are in a moment of gratitude about something you are vibrating at a positive level and giving out emotions of contentment, joy, and peace. As per the Law of Attraction, you will then see more contentment, joy, and peace come into your life. You simply cannot be coming from a place of scarcity while you are busy being grateful. I have the following statement I repeat every day in the shower. "I am very grateful for what I have and I am open to receiving more abundance and prosperity in my life today."

Don't forget, too, the other thing that absolutely magnifies the power of manifesting is being in the Now in the form of play. We all forget as we grow older how to play like we did when we were kids. When you are involved in a moment of play, whether you are playing with the dog, climbing, snowboarding, painting a picture, walking in a rainforest, jet skiing, watching a funny movie—whatever you consider joyful—then you are manifesting at your most powerful. You are in the now and you are in a state of joy.

Next, work as a team. If you are in a family situation, you should take the attitude that you are operating as a team. After all, you are all manifesting together. I take my children everywhere with me on business and have since they were quite a young age. They have sat in on all legal appointments, bank managers meetings, accountants meetings, and so on—anything to do with business. My theory is that if they wish to be successful themselves, the more experience they can gain talking and listening to professionals, the less intimidated they will be when it is their turn to deal with them.

Also, talk about money and spirituality with them openly. It is a shame parents share all sorts of things with their children but often they don't involve them in the family finances or religious discussions. I believe this is a huge mistake. There is a board game developed by Robert Kyosaki called *Cashflow 101*. We get great enjoyment as a family playing this game together. It teaches the fundamentals of investing and cash flow.

Another tip: don't buy into the doom and gloom theories that some people seem to relish in. I cannot count how many times I have heard comments like "the world is getting worse and worse." I don't buy that. Maybe people have forgotten their history from school, but all I can say is I am glad I can't remember living a life at any time over the last couple of thousand years. I personally feel the world is getting better and better every year. We are no longer burnt at the stake for being a witch. We have freedoms of speech not experienced in previous years. Countries are no longer marching into other countries to take them over. Yes, we have trouble in the Middle East and other places in the world, and I look forward to a resolution that satisfies both the Israelis and the Palestinian states, but in previous centuries, rape and pillaging of other countries was the norm rather than the exception. Mass media, and again the Internet, has made the planet a much smaller place. In most countries now women have voting rights, and we are making huge breakthroughs in medicine and technology. At least now, when there is an atrocity, there are people yelling and shouting about it demanding change, unlike hundreds of years ago, when it was accepted quietly.

I could go on and on, but the bottom line is the world is heading the right way. Are we there yet? Well no, we are not wherever "there" is yet, but we have a loud voice working on stamping out poverty. We have leaders worried about the environment. We have social activists fighting for human rights. The tide, I believe, has turned and humanity, jointly, is manifesting a fairer, more peaceful world for all of us.

In the book *Power vs. Force*, mentioned before, by Dr. David R Hawkins, his studies have identified the vibration rate of nearly everything on the planet. Out of interest, the highest vibrating book on the planet is the *Bhagavad-Gita* (the Hindu bible), and the highest vibrating human ever on earth was, you guessed it, Jesus, at around 1,000. In his studies, Dr. David Hawkins claims the level of 200 is the level where, below that, negative attracts more negative; any higher and positive tends to spiral up. For example, hatred and jealousy would be two emotions that vibrate below 200. I am sure we all know people who we think would also vibrate under 200; they feel like black clouds entering a room. Peace, love, and happiness are emotions that vibrate over 200. Dr. Hawkins makes the point that in recent years, humanity itself moved above the 200 mark for the first time ever. Humanity is now vibrating at its highest point ever. This should make all people smile.

On this point, I am sure there are many people who would ask the question, "Why would mankind manifest to itself something like terrorism?" Now, I would not even pretend to know for sure what part terrorism plays in the overall plan; however, I do have one theory which may have something to do with it.

To explain this theory, I would like to track back to the suspected prophet Nostradamus. I am not a student of Nostradamus. There is actually a lot he has said that I don't think has happened. However, I do remember a documentary on the subject, and one of the predictions was about the "mighty war" that would occur at the end of the century and into the new century. It would start just after 1984 and he said it would go for about twenty-seven years. We are right in the timeframe he refers to. I recall that he implied that the world's super powers would all be on the same side. He also said that at the end of the war we would come to an era of peace. I remember at the time discussing this concept with friends. We couldn't imagine what on earth would put the super powers on the same side. We considered crazy theories such as invasion from outer space. I mean, from where we stood at that time, we could not imagine that the United States would be co-operating with the USSR on anything. We were brought up in the middle of the Cold War.

Ironically, recent information has shown that Osama Bin Laden started planning his campaign of terror back around 1985, and of course we have seen the world cooperate in an attempt to stem this hideous violence across the globe. I find it interesting that we have a global war on terror that is uniting governments around the world.

So, in relation to manifesting, why would this be the case, I wonder? Why have we manifested this to ourselves? My theory is that humans have an increased desire to see the planet united as one. It is becoming our deepest desire to end war between nations and to end starvation and poverty. We desire a world that is operating as one, where all people are equal. We desire a world where we are co-operating in overcoming the challenges we have in this reality of relativity.

Hence, I believe, that terrorism is part of the overall plan to unite all nations. The threat of terrorism worldwide has forced nations to cooperate in a way as never seen before. Through this newly found co-operation we can now also address situations such as world poverty, oppression, starvation, international crime, and human slavery.

It is through the individual desire for world peace we will bring upon ourselves experiences that will ultimately move the world in the direction we want it to go. Time has shown that humans bond the best when there is a negative situation to overcome. Perhaps terrorism is the catalyst required to unite the globe and, once united, move it closer to creating the future we are all looking for. Maybe, in the long term, the terrorists themselves will ultimately be responsible for the whole world joining forces and coming from one voice: a voice of peace.

Again, it comes down to trusting the universe. If each human works on just what he or she is putting out into the universe, then eventually a time will come when we will see the world peace we so desire. As I have said a few times, the potential for all is available in this world, but it doesn't mean we have to manifest the truly negative into the physical reality. The more we put forward the desire for a united, peaceful world, the more we will manifest situations that are compatible with that desire.

It's about playing the game. You want to participate and experience it while being aware that you don't have to participate if you don't want to. The level of involvement you have in society is always your call. Don't take things so personally and always observe the motives behind what is making people respond the way they are. Above all, stop judging; just observe and react accordingly.

Remember too that in the end we are all one. Every one of us comes from the same eternal source of energy, and every one of us, without exception, chose to come to this place of relativity.

Treat all people with respect, not because the Law of Attraction demands you should if you want to receive respect in your life but because you do not know what that person's journey involves or what they are trying to achieve. Many people choose not to see the simplicity in life yet because they are still knee deep in the illusion of the whole thing. They may not be ready to accept that it is an illusion and take responsibility for the reality they have. Leave them be. We are not here to convert. We are here to share, support, and help. They will live their reality the way that it needs to be for them.

In serious cases, where someone's negativity becomes too intense, I just walk away. Turn the other cheek, so to speak. Maybe in a couple of years they will have a greater understanding of who they are, but until that time, you stay over there and I will live my life over here and all will be good. You have nothing to gain by pointing out (what you have decided) their weaknesses are to them. I respect every person's right to live their life as they choose, either with or without all the drama, power plays, and complaining. I just don't have to be included.

It is worth noting that the original definition of the word Armageddon translates to "the revealing of a secret." When I heard that, it gave me goose bumps. There are many writings these days that have been supposedly channelled in from the other side that talk about the revealing of the secret. The secret being who we are, why we are here, and how we are able to manifest anything we want in the world into our reality. These writings say that more and more people are finding themselves with intuition and psychic powers than ever before in history, and this may be true.

Could it be that the world is not going to blow itself up or have a fiery dramatic end, as so many scriptures seem to suggest? Maybe it could be as simple as we all wake up from this "dream" and realise we all have the powers that Jesus Christ had, and we start using them. Take away the fear and you will take away most of the evil that exists in this reality.

CHAPTER 19

FINAL THOUGHTS

Let's go over this one more time.

- You are an eternal soul who normally resides in heaven. You are not a human having a spiritual experience; you are a spirit having a human experience.

- The only reason you are here is to experience relativity. If you do nothing more than that, and then return home, you have achieved all that you set out to do. You are a human just being!

- You are unconditionally loved by the universe, your guides, angels, and loved ones. They are there to help you wherever possible. All you have to do is ask.

- There is nothing to prove. There is nothing to be earned. You will get to go home when the time is right.

- Through your experiences you will create preferences, which, when sharpened, become your desires.

- The universe brings to you your sharpest desires on a conscious, subconscious, and super-conscious level through the Law of Attraction.

- The Law of Diminishing Return guarantees that you will continually change your preferences and desires.

- It is through you overcoming your own challenges that your greatest pride is felt, hence you further define yourself and who you are.

- It is virtually impossible for you to understand what is good or bad, because the Law of Relativity, the Law of Attraction, and the Law of Diminishing Return are operating on a conscious, subconscious and super-conscious level at all times.

- The universe answers what you put out through your thoughts words and actions, every time, without fail.

- Free will gives you the ability to put your preference and desires forward however, fate takes a hand in bringing those desires to you.

- Trust that the universe and your higher self understands what you need better than you do, but participate in the process of co-creating your reality on a daily basis.

- Remember that we are all one. We all come from the one source and we have all volunteered to come here.

Finally, work with an attitude of cooperation rather than competition. This is a game; it is a team game. Every single thought and action you have affects every other person and therefore ultimately you. Until we learn to work as *Team Humanity* we will not be able to minimise the negativity we see in our lives and on a global basis.

I hope there has been something in this book for you. I hope you, like me, can take this understanding and use it to create a more peaceful existence. Do I still get cranky and such? Sure I do. I am certainly no saint. There are still things that upset me like wet washing on rainy days, running out of money before the weeks out, the media misrepresenting a situation, and nearly anything else when I am really tired or out of coffee.

Do I still get upset with what's happening in our world? I certainly do. With paedophiles and rapists out there hurting young children, who wouldn't be sad? However, the level of fear, the level of worry, and the level of stress is so considerably lower, and the feelings of peace, happiness, and love are much more prevalent than ever before.

I may not be able to change the whole world singlehandedly, but I can participate in working with the rest of humanity to make it slightly better, and then slightly better again, until one day, maybe, we won't have to deal with as much relativity as we do today. If you can just get rid of a little bit of the fear, the anger, the frustration and the sadness that exists on a day to day basis in your life, then you too are contributing towards making the world a better place.

Will we ever be able to fix it completely? No, I imagine not. I don't think that is the goal. There is nothing to fix. We certainly do not want a sterile society. The whole point of this place is to experience the positive and the negative of the situation over our lifetime so we can define ourselves. I do think, though, that it doesn't have to be quite this negative, and we can actively participate in keeping some of that negativity out of our lives by consciously being aware of what thoughts we are putting out into the universe. If we work within ourselves first, then we can step out and help the rest of the world as well.

I am hopeful that you have found some answers to your search for meaning in this "interesting" world. It is not easy. It was not designed to be. However, we do have a connection to that divine power that controls the whole scene and we also have the ability to decide ourselves what comes into our reality.

There is one word used more than any in this book, and that is the word trust, and that is because peace always comes down to trust.

Trust yourself.
Trust the universe.
Trust life.

I wish you all the best in your life. The world is truly a wonderful place!